MAKING A MEAL OF IT

MAKING A MEAL OF IT

Rethinking the Theology of the Lord's Supper

Ben Witherington III

BAYLOR UNIVERSITY PRESS

Cover Design by Jeremy Reiss

Witherington, Ben, 1951-
Making a meal of it : rethinking the theology of the Lord's Supper /
Ben Witherington III.
    p. cm.
Includes index.
ISBN 978-1-60258-015-2 (cloth : alk. paper)
1. Lord's Supper. I. Title.

BV825.3.W58 2007
234'.163--dc22

                                    2007028564

Printed in the United States of America on acid-free paper with a
minimum of 30% pcw recycled content.

For Tom and Maggie

Faithful friends and faithful servants of our Savior

CONTENTS

PREFACE

This is the second volume of a trilogy of little books on those basic elements of Christian life and worship that all Christians take far too much for granted—I am referring to the sacraments of baptism and the Lord's Supper, and the Word of God. In some ways, these are the very elements that Christians worldwide share most in common. It thus behooves us to understand them and approach these "means of grace" in as careful and prayerful a manner as is possible, and indeed in as biblical a manner as is possible. As with the previous study, we will be working through crucial New Testament passages, here ones that deal with the Lord's Supper. We will also be studying the Lord's Supper in its social context, asking whether it was part of a larger meal in the time of the first-century church, and if so, what that means. We must begin, however, where we began with the study of baptism—discussing the Jewish antecedents of this ritual. As we shall see, there is a relationship between Passover, the Last Supper, the Lord's Supper, and indeed even the Lamb's Supper, and at least the last three of these meals all share in common the idea that communion with God, perhaps even some sort of union with God, is what the meal is all about. Unfortunately our approach to the Lord's Supper in the modern church ranges from the magical on one end of the spectrum to the trivial on the other. The truth about this ceremony lies somewhere in-between. But perhaps we may start with a couple of stories.

The phone rang and there was an angry priest at the other end of the line. At the time I was just the caretaker of a small Methodist church in South Hamilton, Massachusetts. I was not even ordained at that juncture. It was a Sunday morning and there had been a wedding in a nearby small Catholic church involving both Methodists and Catholics the previous evening. The priest who was the pastor of that church had not been involved or present at the wedding on that Saturday. In fact, the service had been officiated by one Methodist minister and one Catholic priest whom the priest in question really did not know. The voice at the other end of the line said with some irritation: "I have all these hosts lying on the altar, and I need to know if they have been consecrated or not." It took me a minute to realize he was talking about the communion wafers. I asked why he was so concerned. His reply floored me: "If they have been consecrated, then, of course, they are quite literally the body of Christ, and if so, I must now consume them all or else we will have profaned the body of Christ." Indeed, he had to do so even if he was not sure if they had been consecrated or not. Someone had been careless with the wafers and left them on the small altar in that church. When I told the priest I honestly did not know if the wafers had been consecrated, I could hear an audible groan at the other end of the line, and then he hung up. It was going to be an unusual second breakfast for that priest on that Sunday morning.

The seeker-friendly megachurch in a larger northern city had decided to try an innovative approach to the Lord's Supper. Everyone present would be invited to partake. And they decided to use unusual elements—after all, this was a service where one came casual and the whole approach to the matter was casual. So they made up a large batch of Kool-Aid and brought in some tasty crackers of one sort or another.

And in the middle of the service "communion" was served. At the end of the service one first-time guest came up to the minister, shook his hand, and said, "You know what I liked best about the service?" "No," said the minister, "do tell me." She said, "I liked that you stopped what you were doing and we all had snacks in the middle. That was very nice." The minister, a bit taken aback, had an unacceptable image flash through his head—"This is my snack, given for you."

These stories compellingly bring to light an important fact: Christians today have widely divergent views of the Lord's Supper and what happens when one takes it. And to some degree this is because we have all moved a considerable distance from what the New Testament actually says about the Lord's Supper. Though there is more discussion about the Lord's Supper in the New Testament, at least in 1 Corinthians, than there is about baptism, the remarks are still tantalizingly brief and agonizingly incomplete. It will be in order, then, to reexamine the source material.

But let me say right out of the box that I am afraid that most denominations have, to use a British idiom, "made a meal" out of the Lord's Supper, not in the positive sense of the phrase but in the sense of having "made a mess" out of the sacrament, busily ignoring it altogether in some quarters, treating it as a mere symbol in others, or treating it as if saying "*hoc est meum corpum*" really is some sort of hocus pocus, some sort of magical act that transforms the elements into something they were not before. In fact, did you know that the phrase hocus pocus comes to us as a barbarizing of the Latin phrase for "This is my body"? How have we come so far from the Last Supper meal and what it entailed? Inquiring minds need to know. Hopefully this study will help us sort out such vital questions once more, or at least begin to do so. If not, some of us are going to continue to get indigestion contemplating what we seem to be doing to the Lord's Supper.

—Easter 2007

Chapter 1

PASSED OVER, PAST DUE

A group of rabbis get together to discuss whether it was necessary to go all the way to Jerusalem to celebrate Passover. The debate goes on at length and finally they take a vote. All the rabbis but one agree that it is necessary to make the journey to Jerusalem for Passover. The rabbi who disagrees will not change his mind; in fact he calls on the Bat' Qol [the daughter of a voice—i.e. the voice of God speaking from heaven] *to speak directly to the meeting to confirm that he is right that it is fine to have the Passover celebration in their little village. The Bat' Qol speaks and says that it is fine for the Passover to be celebrated in the village. The same rabbis then proceed to take another vote, and they vote to rule the Bat' Qol out of order, and off they go to Jerusalem!*

—Variant tradition of BT Baba Metzia 59B

Neither the celebration of Passover nor the celebration of early Jewish communal meals nor the celebration of the Last Supper nor the celebration of the Lord's Supper could by any stretch of the imagination be called entrance rituals, unlike baptism or circumcision. To the contrary, all these rites and practices were ways of strengthening already

1

existing bonds between God and his people, and among those people themselves. And, of course, those bonds needed to be strengthened regularly, and so these became repeatable and repeated practices. They were not about initial union, but rather ongoing communion.

It is certainly true that there were not nearly as many possible antecedents for the practice of the Lord's Supper as there were for Christian baptism. This does not mean that the debate in Christian circles down through church history has been any less contentious when it came to the Lord's Supper than it was about baptism, but it does mean that the historical issues are somewhat clearer for the Lord's Supper. For one thing, we don't have to deal with the practices of John the Baptizer and his followers. Nothing suggests there was a meal ritual that Jesus or his followers derived from John and his devotees. So where should we start the discussion of the possible antecedents of the Lord's Supper? The answer must be with the Jewish celebration of the Exodus-Sinai delivery.

REMEMBERING THEIR BONDAGE:
THE PASSOVER CELEBRATION

Sometimes I get a little peeved with the way my denomination celebrates the Lord's Supper, by which I mean the infrequency of the ritual. By tradition it was to happen once a quarter, because that's how often the ordained circuit riders could show up in a parish and serve it in the eighteenth and nineteenth centuries. We are doing it more like once a month these days. But when I get frustrated, I remember that it took the Israelites some forty years after leaving Egypt before they first celebrated Passover in the promised land (Josh 5). What's most interesting about that whole story is that they began to celebrate the meal in the land once the manna from heaven, which sustained them in the wilderness, ceased to be given. There is something suggestive about that, more than just that all God's children need to eat! The Passover meal is not about the "bread of heaven" but about the "bread of haste" and what happened in the Exodus events themselves.

Oddly enough, the English word Passover comes to us not from Jewish quarters but from the great English translator of the Bible, William Tyndale. It was apparently Tyndale who coined the word Passover as a term that sounded something like the Hebrew pesah. In some respects Christians have the same trouble distinguishing the Last Supper from the Lord's Supper that early Jews sometimes had distinguishing the events of the Passover in Egypt recorded in Exodus 12:1-13 from the later celebration of those events as recorded in Exodus 12:14-23 (cf. Deut 16:1-8). And then of course there is the further problem that this Passover celebration continued to develop in form through the centuries, adding things like a chair for Elijah, the matzo balls and more.

The basic story of the original event in Egypt is familiar enough and has been dramatized enough (e.g. in the movie *The Ten Commandments*) for many moderns to assume they know the story and its significance. But it will be well if we revisit the story once more and consider its significance. What we will discover is that it is not a story about an atoning sacrifice by means of the offering of a lamb. The ritual of the blood on the lintel of the door, which protected the Israelites from the angel of death, is an *apotropaic* (avoidance) ritual, such that the family in question would be "passed over" by the aforementioned denizen of death. Later Jewish and Christian ideas that amalgamated this story with ideas about the scapegoat's providing a substitutionary remedy should not be read into the original tale. The scapegoat symbolized the removal of sin from the nation and perhaps the judging of a substitute. The blood of the Passover lamb on the door symbolized not a sacrifice for sin but rather protection from divine judgment. There is a difference. Let us consider some of the details of the Passover stories.

It will be useful to offer a couple of quotes from the Passover Seder ceremony at this point. The ceremony basically begins with a child asking the elders at the table, "Why is this night special above all other nights?" Normally it is the father who responds by telling the ancient story. Notice the "we were there" element in the storytelling itself:

> We were Pharaoh's slaves in Egypt, and the Lord our God brought us forth from there with a mighty and an outstretched arm. And if the Holy One, blessed be he, had not brought our forefathers forth from Egypt, then we, our children and our children's children, would still be Pharaoh's slaves in Egypt. . . . And the more one tells the story of the departure from Egypt, the more praiseworthy is he. . . . In each generation let each one look on himself as if he came forth from Egypt. As it said: "And you shall tell your son in that day, saying: 'It is because of that which the Lord did for me when I came forth from Egypt.'"

Notice that the rehearsal of the story makes clear that it is not just a matter of Jews' remembering who they were, but indeed who they are and continue to be. There is a corporate solidarity of Jews in these events over many generations.

It is fair to say that the Passover is an event and a cultic celebration that has special significance not only for Jews but also for Christians. Some Christians today might well ask: how is this the case, since as Christians we are not under the old covenant? Several answers may be given. For one thing, the death of Jesus as recounted in all four canonical gospels is set against the backdrop of the Passover celebration in April of A.D. 30 (or possibly 33). Furthermore, as Brevard Childs points out, "not only did the issue of Passover become a burning controversy in early Christian history, but the Passover became a vehicle for almost every important Christian doctrine with the controversy ensuing from the early Middle Ages throughout the post-Reformation period."[1] In some senses the debate was still raging in the late twentieth century as can be seen by the vigorous discussion by Joachim Jeremias of whether the Last Supper was in fact a Passover meal or not.[2]

It must be admitted that there is a certain ambivalence in the way New Testament writers approach the Jewish Passover traditions. Clearly enough some early Jewish Christians continued to celebrate Passover well after Jesus' death, and to judge from 1 Corinthians 11, this practice was exported by Paul to his own mostly Gentile communities in places like Corinth, or at least the language and imagery of that celebration was used in the context of the Christian meal. But on the other hand, when it began to be concluded by Paul and the Beloved Disciple, and perhaps others that Jesus was himself the Passover lamb who brought that ceremony to fulfillment and completion, the question would naturally be asked whether there was a point in celebrating something that was now seen as but a foreshadowing or a type of the great Christ event. Notice how on the one hand the Synoptics depict Jesus as apparently eating the Passover, while in John 13 there is no such implication; and, in fact, we had already been told in John 1 that Jesus is the Lamb of God, who takes away the sins of the world in and by himself. It thus behooves us to examine the material in Exodus 12 and also 13:17-22.

Notice, first of all, that Exodus 12:1-3 suggests from the outset that this is not something celebrated in a cultic context but rather in a family and home context. It must have been a home ritual long before it ever was a temple ritual involving priestly sacrifice. There is perhaps evidence in Exodus 12:14-20 that the earlier material is being edited in light of the later Jewish celebration itself. In fact, traditional Jewish exegesis has seen Exodus 12:1-13 as reflecting the original Passover as it was uniquely celebrated in Egypt, while verses 14ff. were thought to reflect the later and perpetual ordinance. It is also possible that there were unleavened-bread rites and new-moon sacrifices celebrated by the Israelites before the Sinai events, but whatever rites they may have had before, it appears likely that during the course of the Exodus-Sinai events at a minimum such rituals were given a new reference and meaning connected with those historical occasions. As Childs says, verses 1-13 are describing the Passover in terms of its chronological sequence, while verses 14-20 are concerned with the length of time for the ritual. The upshot of this is that we are meant to view both Passover and Massot (Unleavened Bread) as part of one redemptive event, and so verses 1-20 should be treated as a whole, though it has two parts.

From the beginning of Exodus 12 it is stressed that, unlike the other of Israel's ordinances, Passover and Unleavened Bread were instituted in Egypt. Verse 2 indicates that the new Israelite calendar is to date from the time of these very events. The month in question was called Abib and seems to correspond to our March-April, though they were later to call the month Nisan (Exod 13:4; 23:15; Deut 16:1).[3] This meant that Passover became a spring festival, not because it superceded some former spring festivals but because the original events transpired in the spring.

In verse 3 we have the crucial term *edah*. It refers to the "gathering" or congregation of God's people. We do not find the more usual term *qahal* here, which some have seen as the origin of the New Testament term *ekklesia* since both terms refer to a special assembly of some sort. The term gathering or congregation does not refer to an abstraction here but rather to an actual physical meeting or coming together of God's people for a religious purpose. This celebration was not optional but was to involve the whole people of God. It took place house by house, and the head of the house was responsible for supplying the sacrificial animal.

The Hebrew word *seh* is used here to refer to the animal to be used, and in fact this is a neutral term that alludes to a head of small stock, whether a sheep or goat only the context makes clear. There is no limitation of age inherent in this Hebrew term either. That limitation we derive from the phrase "son of a year," which is used to describe the animal. This presumably means an animal born within the last year. We may assume it was a lamb since the kid was used less frequently for actual sacrifice, especially when a special occasion was in view.

The fact that in Exodus 12 the rite is depicted as a family one strongly argues for its authenticity and originality, for we do not see the later temple interests and hegemony intruding here. Each household was to have its own celebration, unless a household was too small to eat the whole animal, in which case another small family would be invited to share the food and occasion. The animal was to be unblemished, and it was to be slaughtered in the evening and eaten on the same evening. The roasting over an open fire also suggests the primitiveness of this narrative, for it indicates that the Israelites were still in their seminomadic state of existence. They had not yet settled down in the promised land and bought their gas grills for the backyard! Notice how what is said here contrasts with Deuteronomy 16:7. Here in Exodus the animal is to be roasted; there to be boiled. The latter reflects later practical and hygienic considerations intervening in the ceremony.

At this juncture it is important to say something about Exodus 12:7. This verse implies that we are dealing with a ritual that did *not* involve atoning for sin, but rather *was* a rite of protection for God's people, a different though not unrelated matter. It involved a blood ritual to avoid God's last blow against the firstborn. Thus Passover and atonement were not originally associated, though apparently by Jesus' day there were some such associations. Notice that nothing at all is said or suggested here about Israel's sin, or about forgiveness. This ceremony is more like an insurance policy. Yes, the blood is to avert divine wrath, but it is not wrath against Israel's particular sins. In this case they simply happened to be too close to the danger zone, or in the line of fire. We must assume that this blood ritual arose before there even was a fully formed priesthood, for it is highly unusual to have such a ritual without any mention of involvement of priests.

The celebration also involves bitter herbs and unleavened bread. The Hebrew term *massot* is the source of the term "matzos" today. We might do better to translate here "unleavened cakes," which is still a staple of Bedouin diet today. *Merorim* is the word translated "bitter herbs" and may refer to a wild lettuce of sorts. The Mishnah was later to include five herbs in its list of acceptable and useable wild plants for this ritual (lettuce, chicory, pepperwort, snakeroot, and even dandelion). According to later Jewish tradition the bitter herbs symbolized the bitterness of bondage (cf. Exod 1:14) but nothing is said of that here in Exodus 12. Similarly the massot later came to be called "the bread of haste" obviously symbolizing the haste the Israelites had to make when leaving Egypt all of a sudden and thus having no time to put leaven into the dough and let it rise. As verse 11 says, they were to eat fully dressed and packed to run when the order came down. The original Passover turns out to be the ancient equivalent of military MREs—meals ready to eat!

Verse 12 tells us that the judgment of Yahweh is not only on the Egyptians but also on their deities. This is probably an allusion to the fact that Egyptians would often pray for the safety of their firstborn, particularly firstborn sons, as was the custom in many ancient patriarchal cultures. The death of the firstborn would be seen as a sign of the anger or perhaps the impotence of their gods. This is worth pondering when it comes to the death of Jesus as God's only begotten, or beloved, Son. Would Jesus' contemporaries have assumed his death was a manifestation of God's wrath? Probably so. In any event, Yahweh is showing his superiority over the spirits behind the pagan deities, and thus we should not overlook the supernatural struggle that is implied to be behind the contest of wills between Moses and Pharaoh.

This leads us to discuss the term *pesah* itself. Today, of course, it is usually translated "Passover," but that rendering actually only goes back to William Tyndale as we have mentioned. Note two things: (1) the verbal form of this word occurs at verse 13 and gives us the origin of the term, a verb that is partially explained by the second half of verse 13—no blow will fall on Israel; therefore they have been passed over. The verbal form here is *pasah*, which is obviously related to *pesah*, the noun form, and not to other connotations of that verb where it refers to limping (cf. 2 Sam 4:4), much less a limping dance supposed to be associated with the ritual; and (2) clearly the sense *pass over* suits the context here (vv. 13:23, 27; cf. Isa 31:5). It is worth stressing that the concept here is that God passed his people over, not that God overlooked them. Notice immediately the difference in the ongoing ritual spoken of in verses 14-20. In the latter text we hear about the Israelites eating massot for a week (vv. 15-16). The events in Egypt hardly permitted such a thing.

Perhaps a word here on leaven is in order. Leaven was usually a piece of old fermented dough used as a starter, a rising agent for the next batch of bread. In other words, it was leftovers. This may suggest one reason why the symbolism of unleavened bread was so potent. It referred to God's people having a fresh start, involving a new calendar, a new freedom, and a whole new way to commemorate God's dealings with them. It is not surprising then that leaven became a symbol of corruption (cf. Matt 16:11; 1 Cor 5:6-8), especially when it began to be distinguished from yeast, a healthier rising agent. In fact, in Leviticus 2:11 and 6:17 leaven seems to be frowned upon.

Notice that verse 11 tells us that this Passover is the Lord's, which likely means we have here a Passover sacrifice for Yahweh, but it may also suggest that Yahweh is he who has both instigated these events and this new set of rites to go with the new set of circumstances. We could compare Yahweh's Passover with the terminology of the Lord's Supper. Just how serious this ritual was is indicated by verse 15 where we hear that anyone who does not observe the unleavened rule will be cut off, which presumably means expelled from the community rather than killed. This demonstrates the importance and seriousness of proper observance of this memorial to the events that led to the exodus and freedom and the covenanting at Sinai.

Verse 22 adds a detail we did not learn at 12:7, namely that the blood is to be put on the doorposts with a bunch of hyssop. Hyssop is a small bushy plant that may be the same as Syrian majoram, and it made a good sprinkler of liquids when fastened in a bunch. It came to be used in various cultic rites (cf. Lev 14:4ff.; Num 19:6ff.). The alert student of the Gospels will immediately think of the reference to hyssop in John 19:29, where Jesus is given a drink using a bunch of hyssop, yet one more hint that the author sees Jesus as being the Passover Lamb. Compare how in Mark's account of the crucifixion he mentions Jesus' being offered wine mixed with myrrh, which was certainly a bitter herb (cf. Mark 15:23 and 1 Cor 5:7). In Exodus 12:23b we have a reference to the "destroyer," perhaps an allusion to the angel of death (cf. 2 Sam 24:16), though at verse 13 it appears to be God in person. But often God and his messenger are interchangeable figures in this literature, for the action of God's agent is seen as the action of God in person. We have a clever wordplay at verse 23 between Passover (*pesah*) and door (*pethah*). As is only appropriate after all this, the Israelites respond with a sign of worship—bowing down before Yahweh.

It needs to be stressed at this point that the celebration of Passover during and well before Jesus' era was not seen as the mere celebrating of a memorial meal of purely symbolic value. When we hear about the current celebrants' considering themselves part of the original exodus story (a sort of "we were there" feature) such that they were among those delivered from bondage in Egypt, we see how this meal serves to strengthen the ethnic bond with previous generations of Jews, including the foundational members of the group. Thus *anamnesis* is more than remembering; it is a placing of current Jews into the ancient story such that it is and becomes once again their own story, their own trial and triumph, which took place in the Exodus-Sinai events. As we shall see, something similar can be said about the Lord's Supper as well.

Since all the earliest Christians were Jews, it is not a surprise that the celebration of Passover likely continued in Christian contexts, particularly in the Holy Land, but at some juncture it seems, even in Jerusalem, to have been superceded, or at least overshadowed, by the celebration of the Lord's Supper. How was this transition made, and what elements of carry-over were there? To answer this question, we need to consider carefully the issue of meals, especially ceremonial meals, in early Judaism, for it appears that for some time the Christians celebrated the Lord's Supper in the context of a meal.

"THOU PREPAREST A TABLE BEFORE ME"— THE SOCIAL NATURE OF MEALS IN EARLY JUDAISM AND EARLY CHRISTIANITY

Social historians have taught us a great deal of late about closely examining ancient rituals and ceremonies and being able to distinguish the two. A ritual, technically speaking, is something that is practiced only once on a particular person or group of persons and frequently deserves the label "rite of passage." Good examples of these would be a circumcision rite, a bar mitzvah, an ordination ritual, the manumission and enfranchising of a slave as a freedman who thus becomes a Roman citizen, and of course Christian baptism.[4] In each case the rite marks the crossing of a boundary that can be properly crossed only once. Rites of passage make clear the difference between the in-group and the outsiders, between the clean and the unclean, between members and nonmembers, between youths and adults, between slavery and freedom, between noncitizens and citizens, and between one religious group and another. Properly speaking, marriage as well is meant to be a ritual or rite of passage, not a ceremony, for the latter is something that is not merely repeatable but is intended to be repeated. It is a sign of the confusion of our times that we speak of a Christian marriage ceremony, rather than the marriage ritual, even though it has the clause "until death do us part" and is said to involve a one-flesh union that is irrevocable.

By contrast with a ritual, ceremonies are intended to be repeated. While the ritual of baptism can symbolize the initial passage into the people of God by an outsider, the Lord's Supper is not intended to function in this fashion, any more than Passover was for Jewish persons. The latter are ceremonies of communion or reunion, not rites of initial union. Rituals by definition are about status change, status reversal, status transformation, whilst ceremonies are about status confirmation, including the confirmation of roles one plays within the in-group. To put it another way, baptism is a group-creating ritual, whilst Passover or the Lord's Supper is a group sustaining or renewing ceremony.

It is not an accident that rituals and ceremonies tend to be administered differently. The former tends, though not always, to involve a passive recipient. No one circumcises or baptizes oneself, ordains oneself, or naturalizes oneself, or if one does, it is not seen as valid. Rather, a gate keeper, someone who monitors the boundary of the community, the society, the guild, or the nation must perform the rite on the recipient. For example, a priest was involved in the manumission ceremony of a slave, not merely the owner and the slave himself in the Greco-Roman world. The fiction involved was the notion that a god was redeeming or ransoming the slave at a cost. By contrast, a ceremony involves one or more active participants and is something shared regularly by the in-group. The elements or actions of a ceremony must be freely taken up or consumed in the ceremony. There were of course quite normally prerequisites to participating in either rituals or ceremonies in antiquity, and these varied precisely because the social functions of rituals and ceremonies differed. For example, while Passover or the Lord's Supper can be said to be a ceremony of *koinōnia*, of active participation or sharing something in common with others, this is not usually the case with rituals, which are performed by one party for another.

Social historians have also reminded us of another crucial point—rituals and ceremonies depict and encode at least some of the major values of the community that practices these exercises.[5] We can learn much about the belief and behavior structure that is at the heart of early Judaism and early Christianity by asking questions like: What is depicted and said about rituals such as circumcision or baptism on the one hand and ceremonies such as Passover or the Lord's Supper on the other? What *values* are inculcated by these procedures? For example, it is no accident that both circumcision and Passover are associated with group-founding events—the inauguration of the Abrahamic covenant or the Exodus-Sinai events. Nor is it an accident that Christian baptism is associated with aspects of Jesus' death and the cleansing from sin; and the Lord's Supper is also associated with Jesus' death and resurrection. Rituals and ceremonies are forms of symbolic proclamation, the Word made visible, of the community's most sacred beliefs and values. In the case of both Judaism and Christianity these sorts of rituals and ceremonies are linked to historical and historic events, events that led to the formation of the community in the first place. They are not in the first instances symbols of generic religious experiences. They have to do with historic covenanting acts and foundational redemption events. In this regard they are very different from various sorts of Greco-Roman religious rituals and ceremonies including the rites of Isis or the Tauroboleum, or the Dionysian rites, or the Mystery rituals.

There is a difference between how rituals and ceremonies function in historically founded and grounded religions and in mythologically grounded ones. But what happens when a meal, or some sort of eating and drinking ceremony, becomes the central symbol of a faith? I use the word "central" advisedly, as boundary rituals are one thing and central ceremonies and symbols another. The latter especially allude to the central values and beliefs of a sect or religious group.

Meals, perhaps more than any other social event in antiquity, encoded the values of a society, or if it was a sectarian meal, of the sect itself. While we might be prone to calling them rules of etiquette, something Ms. Manners might expostulate on, in antiquity the rules and taboos that applied to meals were serious business. They dictated who would be invited to a meal, where they would sit, what they would eat, and the like. Such gatherings had pecking orders, with the elite guests reclining on the best couches and getting the best food, and the less elite guests further from the head couches and the host of the dinner. As Mary Douglas has put it, if "food is treated as a code, the message it encodes will be found in the pattern of social relations being expressed. The message is about different degrees of hierarchy, inclusion, exclusion, boundaries, and transactions across boundaries. . . . Food categories encode social events."[6]

What is important for us to bear in mind is that Judaism and its subsets had been thoroughly Hellenized by the time we get to the New Testament era, and one of the clearest indicators of this is that Jews reclined on couches and took their meals, following various of the Greco-Roman protocols, just like everyone else did in the Roman Empire. Of course the Hellenistic conventions were adopted and adapted by Jews and Christians to suit their own subcultures, but still we must not underemphasize the Hellenistic influence on these practices. Greco-Roman culture had a high degree of social stratification or hierarchial structure, all reinforced by the society's dining customs. Nowhere is the stratification more evident than in some satirical remarks of Martial:

Since I am asked to dinner . . . why is not the same dinner served to me as to you? You take oysters fattened in the Lucrine lake, I suck a mussel through a hole in the shell; you get mushrooms, I take hog funguses; you tackle turbot, but I brill. Golden with fat, a turtledove gorges you with its bloated rump; there is set before me a magpie that has died in its cage. Why do I dine without you although, Ponticus, I am dining with you. . . . Let us eat the same fare. (*Epigram* 3.60)

In general, as we shall see from subsequent chapters, Christian meals, including the Lord's Supper, had elements that worked against the prevailing hierarchy and stratification of society, and in some respects they were different from early Jewish meals in this respect. This is hardly surprising when we have a saying of Jesus like,

When you give a luncheon or a dinner, do not invite your friends or your brothers or your relatives or rich neighbors, in case they may invite you in return, and you would be repaid. But when you give a banquet, invite the poor, the crippled, the lame, and the blind. And you will be blessed, because they cannot repay you, for you will be repaid at the resurrection of the righteous. (Lk 14:12-14)

What Jesus is saying is that he is rejecting the idea of using meals to reinforce reciprocity cycles and, instead, is suggesting that the meals of his followers should be more gracious and less self-serving. We will say more on this in coming chapters.

Furthermore, while the celebration of the Passover was a family event, which did indeed re-encode the parent-child hierarchy in the family, the celebration of the Lord's Supper was a family-of-faith event that involved all Christians coming together to celebrate in someone's home. The home setting was the same as for the Passover meal, but the basic group of invitees or participants differed. So-called fictive kinship had replaced physical kinship, or as I would prefer to put it, family of faith had replaced physical family as the core group doing the celebrating in the Christian setting.

In our next chapter we must consider at some length early Jewish meals in Jesus' day and all those sticky questions about whether the Last Supper was in fact a Passover meal. We must also open up another can of worms, namely, whether the meal spoken of in John 13 is identical with the Last Supper or took place earlier in the week. And furthermore, we must examine the "eucharistic words of Jesus," which were to be carried over into the Lord's Supper celebration in various forms. To be sure, opening up a can of worms is not the most appetizing thing to do when you're discussing meals, but it beats trying to decipher what happened at the Diet of Worms![7]

Chapter 2

FROM THE ESSENES TO JESUS

Most of the ancient world regarded hospitality as a fundamental moral prac-
tice. It was necessary to human well-being and essential to the protection of
vulnerable strangers. Hospitality assured strangers at least a minimum of
provision, protection, and connection with the larger community. It also sus-
tained the normal network of relationships on which a community depended,
enriching moral and social bonds among family, friends and neighbors.

—Christine Pohl

We in America all know very well what it is like to have a Thanksgiving meal. It involves family, perhaps friends as well, and way too
much turkey, gravy, stuffing, and cranberry sauce, and hopefully some
real prayers that give thanks for the bounty. I remember a particular
Thanksgiving dinner at my aunt's house in Statesville, North Caro-
lina, where, as we were all sitting down, she asked my father to pray
impromptu over the meal she had been preparing for many hours.
Somewhat flustered and unprepared, he prayed, "Dear Lord, please
bless our sins and pardon this food in your Son's name. Amen." He

would not soon live down that blessing. But then again too many of our meals, including sometimes the way we celebrate the Lord's Supper, need some pardoning!

HAPPY MEALS AT THE TURN OF THE ERA

There were ancient thanksgiving meals in early Judaism as well. It is difficult at this great a remove to critically assess how much of the Mishnah and the Talmuds reflect Jewish practice prior to the holocaust of the destruction of the temple and the center of Jerusalem in A.D. 70. But clearly it was not the case that Jews came up with thanksgiving meals only after A.D. 70. In fact it has been suggested that the Sabbath evening meal was a sort of thanksgiving meal in Jesus' era. More certainly, there was a *Kiddush*, or thanksgiving, prayer at such a meal. Here is how Joachim Jeremias once described the performance of the Kiddush:

> When the stars appear after sunset the head of the household (on the Sabbath: after lighting the Sabbath candle) says the blessing at the table over the cup of wine, in the midst of his family and guests. Then he himself drinks and after him the other people present. In the case that the Friday afternoon meal lasted until the beginning of the Sabbath or on into the Sabbath itself, the meal was ended and then the *Kiddûs* was inserted into the grace after the meal. In the case of the Passover meal, which was the only meal of the year which began after sunset, the sanctification of the feast took place at the beginning of the meal."[1]

Jeremias goes on to stress that there was no Kiddush meal per se, only a Kiddush prayer that was part of various sorts of meals. This then does not help us much when we are looking for precedents for early Christian practices and insights into the origins of the Lord's Supper.

Possibly more helpful and interesting is the material from the Jewish work known as Joseph and Asenath. Two passages are of relevance.

In J&A 8.5 we hear about Joseph refusing to kiss the Egyptian woman Asenath in greeting because, "It is not right for a man who worships God, who blesses with his mouth the living God, and eats the blessed bread of life and drinks the blessed cup of immortality, and is anointed with the blessed unction of incorruption to kiss a strange woman, who blesses with her mouth dead and deaf idols and eats from their table the bread of strangling and drinks from their libation cup of deceit and is anointed with the unction of destruction" (cf. the Decree in Acts 15 about avoiding worshipping idols and things strangled).

We may compare J&A 15.5 and 16.5-6 where we have similar language about the bread and the cup. What is especially interesting about this material is the reference to both blessing and indeed immortality being benefits of participation in such a meal. The spiritual character of the meal is also made evident from the reaction of Joseph in the quoted material. Though this material comes to us probably from the Jewish community in Alexandria, nevertheless it reminds us of the spiritual associations of meals, both pagan and Jewish (and later Christian), associations that we must not underestimate.

What of the meals that the Qumran community partook? Might they be of some relevance for our discussion? Many scholars have thought so. The texts usually brought forward are 1QS 6.4-6 (which refers to the priest blessing the bread and the wine before the meal), 1QSa 2.17-21 (which says much the same), and Josephus's *Jewish War* 2.131, where the priest in question is depicted as saying a prayer before and after the meal. It will be worth quoting the second of these traditions: "And they gather to the community table . . . and the table of the community is arranged and the *tiros* mixed for drinking, [then] shall [no] one [stretch out] his hand to the first part of the bread and . . . before the priest for [he b]lesses the first part of the bread and the tiros [and stretches out] his hand to the bread before them and after the anointed of Israel [shall str]etch out his hands to the bread . . . the whole assembled community, ea[ch according to] his rank." As one can see, this text is fragmented, and this meal seems to have been viewed as an all-male affair. Nevertheless, as Philip R. Davies and his coauthors suggest, this seems to be a reference to a meal with the Messiah, or a messianic meal of some sort. And it may be of some importance that the Damascus Document seems to have encouraged singleness and celibacy (cf. Matt 19:10-12).[2]

Without over-pressing the connections here, it is important to note that this text comes from an early Jewish sect that was extant during the time of Jesus and had a similar messianic and eschatological orientation in various respects. Our text above involves a blessing of the food and seems to be referring to the setting aside of the first fruits of the meal for God. Since the Qumranites seem to have believed in two messianic figures—one priestly and one kingly—this text likely refers to both, celebrating this meal with that community of the pure. Of course this text then must be seen as prescriptive rather than descriptive, since neither of those figures had shown up by the time this document was written. And herein lies a salient difference with the way Last Supper and, later, Lord's Supper traditions are presented. They are presented with the assumption that the Messiah is in their midst and blessing them already. These later Christian texts do not merely describe a future hope. What these Qumran texts do bear witness to is that in some quarters in early Judaism messianic hopes were high, and meals were seen as one essential part of the *koinōnia* that one would share with the Anointed One who even in this Qumran text was expected to bless the bread and drink.

THE LAST MEAL OF A CONDEMNED MAN

Scholars have been apt to say that the Gospels are Passion Narratives with a long introduction. They have also conjectured that the first part of the gospel story that was actually written down was the Passion Narrative, which of course includes the story of the Last Supper. Of course it is true that Paul in 1 Corinthians 11, writing in about A.D. 51-52 and so some twenty years after Jesus' death, knows of a tradition about "the night in which Jesus was betrayed" and shared a meal with his disciples. It is well to keep clearly in mind that while the Gospels recount the chronologically earlier event of the Last Supper, our earliest reference to the event, so far as the date of the source document is concerned, is in 1 Corinthians 11. Here will be a good place to enter the debate about whether the Last Supper was in fact some sort of Passover meal, even if eaten before the appropriate day.

Some general considerations are in order first. Maurice Casey in his recent monograph has argued at length for an Aramaic substratum to the account in Mark of the Last Supper. That is, he has argued that this account in Mark 14:12-26 reflects translation Greek. He goes on to argue that the account may well have been written down in Aramaic in the 40s, and so within about a decade of the death of Jesus.[3] It is possible then that Mark's account provides us with very early material indeed about this event, presumably from the Jerusalem community where Mark's mother hosted meetings of the early disciples (see Acts 12:12).

The second thing to note is the very peculiar, not to say clandestine, nature of the preparations for the meal in question. Mark 14:12 says that the event in question transpired on "the first day of Unleavened Bread" which is then clarified by the phrase "when the Passover lamb is sacrificed." In other words, we are talking about the day *before* Passover was scheduled to be eaten, namely from sundown Thursday to sundown Friday. Presumably, one might be able to find a lamb that was sacrificed early, right at sundown Thursday, and then partake of the meal immediately thereafter instead of waiting until Friday. This might partly explain the clandestine nature of the preparations for the meal. Remember that Exodus 12:18 told us that the Feast of Unleavened Bread preceded the Passover celebration by a day, so it is clear enough this meal happens prior to the normal celebration of Passover on Friday. I take it that "the first day of Unleavened Bread" refers to Nisan 14, the evening before Passover in A.D. 30.

Note Jesus' cryptic instructions to the disciples to go into the city and find a man carrying a water jug. This must surely be a prearranged signal, as men do not normally do the water carrying in that culture (cf. e.g. John 4). Why the secrecy? Presumably because Jesus has already cleansed the temple and the authorities are on the lookout for him and his followers. By tradition, Jewish pilgrims wanted to partake of the ceremony within the walls of Jerusalem, and various residents were prepared to serve them in their guest rooms. Still the picture of Jesus and his disciples sneaking into the city under the cloak of darkness to partake of a premature Passover meal is striking.

Verse 14 is quite explicit and says that the disciples are to tell the owner of the house in question "The Teacher [no name given] asks, Where is my guest room where I may eat the Passover with my disciples?" Clearly it is assumed that the resident of the house knows which teacher is in view and is prepared to take the risk not only of hosting Jesus at all, but also of raising the hackles of the local authorities by serving the meal early.[4] We must assume that the person in question is one of Jesus' Jerusalem followers but presumably not one *of* the Sanhedrin sympathizers, such as Joseph of Arimathea or Nicodemus, since they would likely have issues with the meal being taken early. Notice as well that the room in question is an upper room and that it is the disciples themselves who must prepare the feast.

As we have noted, the Passover meal was the only Jewish evening meal normally partaken of after sundown, and so Jesus had the advantage of darkness when coming to celebrate his last meal with his disciples. And there can be little or no debate in light of Mark 14:12-14 that our Evangelist assumes this was a Passover meal, even with the irregularities mentioned. If one takes into account the Fourth Gospel, it seems likely that Jesus had a ministry of at least two to three years, and so he made more than one trip up to Jerusalem for this festival during his ministry. Perhaps he had taken the meal at the same house in the previous year, A.D. 29.

Here is another factor which we need to consider in unraveling the mysteries of this text. Romans reckoned time from midnight to midnight, so for them there was an overlap between the Day of Unleavened Bread and the day of the slaughtering of the lambs. Mark seems to have been a gospel written for a Roman audience, and this may explain some of the head scratching about the beginning of this story. Mark is working with two ways of reckoning time, or at least he is cognizant of the two and knows his audience will only likely know the Roman way of reckoning.

Where was the animal sacrificed, and in fact, was there even a lamb involved in the Last Supper, since there is no mention of it at all in the story in Mark 14? In regard to the first matter, lambs were sacrificed for the feast outside of Jerusalem in various places, possibly including nearby Bethlehem where Jesus had relational connections. Rather than assuming a sacrifice and roasting or boiling of the animal within the city walls in defiance of the protocols and without taking the lamb to the priests to perform the rite, we may think that some disciples brought the animal in already prepared, or perhaps they boiled the meat within the house, a less noxious option. It is more difficult to answer why the lamb is not mentioned in the description of the meal. Some have suggested, perhaps correctly, that it is because the Evangelists view Jesus himself as the Passover Lamb. This may be so, but it would not explain why the pregospel tradition in Aramaic would omit this detail.

Mark 14:17 is quite precise as to when Jesus and the disciples showed up for the meal—in the evening. This in itself points to this being a Passover meal. Mark is not interested in recounting a blow-by-blow description of the events of the meal. Rather he begins by saying that the disciples were reclining at table and eating when Jesus revealed he would be betrayed. Of course, this remark is not part of the Passover ritual, and it shows what is really paramount in the mind of Mark. To understand this, we need to say a bit more about how meals were viewed in this era, but note that the text is quite explicit that they were reclining at table, reflecting the Hellenizing of the customs.

The practices of hospitality in the ancient Near East, going back long before Jesus' time and continuing to today, involved the notion that the guest in someone's tent or house was sacrosanct, inviolable. Even if one dined with an enemy, if he were allowed into the meal, he was to be treated with respect and in no way harmed (cf. e.g. Ps 23:5).

Thus the notion of a betrayer at the very table of the Passover, which was in fact a meal where you did not invite enemies, but rather family and close friends, is startling in the extreme and quite naturally upsets the disciples. Jeremias reminds us, "This meal of Jesus with his disciples must not be isolated, but should rather be seen as one of a long series of daily meals they had shared together. For the oriental every table fellowship is a guarantee of peace [cf. Gen 43:25-43; Josh 9:1-15], of trust, of brotherhood. Table fellowship is a fellowship of life."[5]

Verses 19-21 recount the extraordinary discussion that follows, and it has nothing to do with Passover protocol. Notice in verse 20 however there is a reference to the betrayer "dipping bread into the bowl" with Jesus. This likely refers to the use of the bitter herbs as a dip for the bread. But the reference to a betrayer is especially a jolt since Passover was supposed to be the most joyful of meals, not the most sorrowful. Exodus Rabbah 18.11, commenting on Exodus 12:41 says, "This night is one of rejoicing for the whole of Israel."

What is even more disturbing is that in the middle of all this mayhem and angst verse 22 tells us that suddenly Jesus took a loaf of bread (presumably an unleavened cake or flat bread), asked God's blessing on it, and then broke it in pieces and gave it to the disciples. This should sound familiar from the discussion above about the meal at Qumran, but it suits any and all such celebratory Jewish meals where God's blessing would be invoked. But those meals were not foreshadowing a death in symbolic language!

One regular feature of the Passover meal was the explanation, if needed, of the elements involved—the bread of haste, the herbs of bitterness, and the like. We do not have these explanations, but what is crucial to bear in mind is that the disciples were preconditioned to think of those descriptions as symbolic in character—the bread was not really "fast" food or "hasty" pudding; it symbolized getting out of Dodge quickly, so to speak. I mention this in light of what follows. When Jesus hands the broken bread to his various disciples (note that they do not break it for themselves), Mark has Jesus say in the Greek: "Take (it); this is my body." There is a connection being made between the bread, and Jesus' own body. But when would this have come in the course of the meal?

Typically, after the thanksgiving prayer and the blessing of the first cup, the meal began with a preliminary course. The Passover lamb would then be served and the second cup was mixed. But before any such eating, Jesus himself as "head of the family" would have offered a brief meditation including interpretation of the elements of the Passover meal. Jeremias is right that we must see Jesus' new words of interpretation within the context of the old interpretations of elements already given. But those interpretations were given before the meal commenced at all, whereas the new interpretations come later in the meal, according to Mark. The other unusual thing is that apparently Jesus himself does not partake of the special bread and cup that he passes around and gives new interpretations to. The word over the bread shows less variation in the tradition than the word over the cup, as is clear from a comparison of 1 Corinthians 11:24 and Luke 22:19, which seem to reflect one stream of tradition (cf. John 6:51c) and Mark 14:22 and Matthew 26:26, which reflect the other. The first thing to note about the bread word is that it is not said while Jesus is breaking the bread, but rather while he is distributing it to the disciples. As Jeremias makes clear, it is not the breaking of the bread or the pouring out of the wine (i.e. the actions involved) that Jesus is interpreting but the elements themselves. This corresponds well with the nature of the interpretations of the Passover elements in the ceremony in general.

In other words, this first word means "this bread is my body." The phrase in question in the Aramaic was likely *zeh basari* or *den bisri* followed by the blood word in the form *zeh dami* or *den idmi*. Now what is striking about this is the separation of flesh/body and blood with two separate symbols, which implies, as Jeremias suggests, sacrifice. "Each of the two nouns presupposes a slaying that has separated flesh and blood. In other words: *Jesus speaks of himself as a sacrifice.*"[6] It should also be stressed that both bread and blood were symbols of life (hence the phrase "bread of life," and the idea that the life was in the blood). But here Jesus is turning that around to refer to death, which paradoxically is or conveys life. The upshot of this is that Jesus may well be referring to himself as the sacrificial lamb that gives life to those who consume it, but which in its shed blood protects from divine wrath. Adding color to this whole description is the fact that red wine was the wine of choice for Passover, and the baked bread would have something like the brown complexion of a Middle Eastern person's flesh.

The "cup" word is more difficult to sort out since it appears with more variation. It appears likely that this word would be offered at the end of the meal and so be separated in time from the bread word. It would also be associated with the last cup before the ceremony was over, the cup that looked forward to the coming kingdom. Comporting with this interpretation is the fact that Jesus swears a vow of abstinence—"I solemnly declare that I will not drink wine again until . . . I drink it new in the Kingdom" (Mark 14:25 NLT)—looking forward perhaps to the messianic meal perhaps alluded to in the Qumran saying we studied previously (cf. Isa 25:6; 65:13; 1 Enoch 62:14; Bar 29.8). The Markan and Matthean forms of the saying are close, with Matthew simply making things clearer by adding the phrase "for the forgiveness of sins" (26:28). Originally the words as spoken by Jesus were probably "This cup—my blood of the covenant which is poured out for many." This comports with the Passion prediction in Mark 10:45. Luke 22:20 and 1 Corinthians 11:25 making clear that Jesus is referring to the new covenant, which is surely likely, as he is talking about inaugurating a new Passover and hence a new redemptive act that sets people free, this time from sin.

To this, someone also added by Paul's day "do this, as often as you drink it, in remembrance of me" (1 Cor 11:25). It is not impossible that this was originally what Jesus said since Passover was also an *anamnēsis* ceremony. Otherwise, it is difficult to understand why the disciples at some juncture would eventually set up a new ceremony that focused on Jesus exclusively and what his death accomplished, while leaving the Passover ritual behind. We are told in both the Markan and Matthean accounts that after the ceremony some songs were sung, which is but one more pointer that this was a Passover meal, for it was customary to sing some of the Hallel Psalms both before the meal (Pss 113–114) and after it (Pss 115–118).

What we have here then in the Last Supper is an enacted parable, much like ancient, prophetic enacting parables or sign acts. "Jesus made the broken bread a simile of the fate of his body, and the blood of grapes a simile of his out-poured blood. 'I go to death as the true Passover sacrifice,' is the meaning of Jesus' last parable."[7] There is nothing here about the transformation of the elements into something they were not before. Nothing here about the words of interpretation referring to actions rather than the elements themselves. Nor any hint that the disciples thought Jesus meant what he said literally, for they do not run out of the room screaming "cannibalism," since the idea of eating human flesh was abhorrent to early Jews (cf. 1 En 98:11; John 6:5). But what is most telling about all this is that Jesus is in a sense symbolically distributing the benefits of his Passion before it happens! How confident he must have been that God would use his death for good to have at this juncture changed or added to the Passover liturgy and referred it to himself and his coming death in this way. It seems certain that the Last Supper memories would never have been turned into a ceremony at all if there had not been something redemptive that happened to Jesus beyond his death—namely, his resurrection. Why else would one want to remember the night one's master was betrayed and all the Twelve failed him—unless there was a sequel without equal and the Eleven were later restored by Jesus? Finally we should bear in mind that Jesus seems to have seen this ceremony as a time to indirectly announce that he was inaugurating a new covenant in his death, a new covenantal relationship between God and his people. And all such covenants were inaugurated with a sacrifice, for it is not just blood but the shedding of blood, life poured out in death, that inaugurates a new relationship while atoning for sin. No wonder Jesus said he longed to share this particular Passover with his family of faith—his disciples. It will be well if at this juncture we go one more mile in this chapter and ask about the earliest recorded meals of Jesus' followers after the crucifixion before turning to the issue of the later celebration that came to be called the Lord's Supper.

"ALL THINGS IN COMMON"—ACTS 2 AND 4

Acts 2:42-47 is the first of the famous summary passages in Acts, the second of which is in Acts 4:32-37; both have produced no end of scholarly speculation.[8] One of the more frequent speculations is the degree to which these first two passages may suggest that the earliest Christians may have been influenced by the communal practices at Qumran. One such balanced discussion is Brian Capper's, with which we will interact briefly here. The overall drift of Capper's argument is that while there are some idealistic and stylized elements in these summaries (which in any case describe the past, not Luke's present, noting the "they used to . . ." verbs in the deponent), nevertheless they do reflect actual historical practice to a real degree. Capper believes there is evidence of "Essene" influence, perhaps from the Essene quarter in Jerusalem, on the earliest Jewish Christians as described in Acts 2 and 4, such that these summaries do indeed depict the historical character of the earliest Christian community. For our purposes what is important about that conclusion is that these summaries refer to some sort of sharing of property including the sharing of meals and making sure no one was in physical need (cf. Acts 5-6).[9]

First of all Capper agrees that Acts 2:44 and 4:32, reflecting the language sometimes used in Greek philosophy to talk about an ideal society—the phrases "all things in common" and "one heart and one soul"—point in this direction (cf. the numerous references he cites to Plato, Aristotle, Aristophanes, Euripides, and other sources).[10] This is in no way surprising since Luke is trying to present a winsome and rhetorically effective portrait to a Gentile patron, Theophilus. As Capper goes on to add, however—though the description is idealistic—in fact Luke is describing something the earliest Christians really attempted. What is less clear is whether or not this involved some sort of communal collection and distribution of goods from a central source, or if it simply involved making sure no one in the Jerusalem community of Christians was in need, as needs arose. Acts 5 and 6 seem to suggest the latter, particularly the story about the neglected Aramaic-speaking widows. But where did the earliest followers of Jesus get the idea of communal living? Surely it did not come from their studying Aristotle or Plato!

Capper therefore suggests the Essenes could have influenced various of these Christians. Philo, Josephus, and even Pliny the Elder all attribute a communal lifestyle to the Essenes (cf. Philo, *That Every Good Man* 75–91; *Hypothetica* 1–18; Josephus, *J.W.* 2.119–161; *Ant.* 18.18–22; Pliny the Elder, *Nat. Hist.* 5.17.4). The Qumran documents themselves suggest a series of phases gone through by a candidate for membership in the community at the end of which, if he wanted to be fully in, he would surrender his property (cf. 1QS 6.18-20 to 6.13-17 and 6.21-23). We have already discussed the meals, including the messianic banquet passage that the Qumran documents spoke about. But just as we would not expect the earliest Galilean and Judean followers of Jesus to have read Plato, so we would not expect them to have read the Qumran documents either. How did the influence happen historically, if it did, or was it just Luke who knew about such ideal notions?

Capper reminds us that there was indeed an Essene Gate in Jerusalem on the south side of the city (see Josephus, *J.W.* 5.145 cf. 2.147–149) not far from Mt. Zion, where the followers of Jesus seem to have congregated (in the "upper room").[11] That there was likely to be contact between these groups so close together in the city seems likely and all the more so since Peter and others spoke in Solomon's portico in the temple from time to time. It is telling that the daily distribution mentioned in Acts 6:1 sounds a good deal like what we find in Philo's description of the Essenes in *Hypothetica* 11.4-11. Bearing these things in mind, let us consider what is said in Acts 2 and 4 in so far as it mentions meals.

It has often been remarked that Luke nowhere directly mentions the Lord's Supper as such in his entire second volume. What should we make of this? Here is where we note that this is the second volume of a two-volume work written to and for Theophilus, and this person will have already heard about the Last Supper referred to in Luke 22. Furthermore, he will have heard the story about the breaking of bread Jesus shared with his disciples at the inn on the road to Emmaus (Luke 24:23 cf. 24:41-42). Then, too, Acts 2:42 and 46 and 20:7 and 11 all suggest that this sort of breaking of bread took place in the context of an act of communal gathering and worship once the community of Christ began to be formed after Easter.[12] Such times together involved praying, teaching, singing, and eating in homes. On the whole then, a good case can be made that "the breaking of bread" was Luke's short-hand for the special Christian meal that came to be called the Lord's Supper by the time Paul wrote 1 Corinthians. The earliest Christian meetings then were characterized not just by acts we would today associate with worship, but also by sharing meals in common and indeed other kinds of property as well. Luke especially had highlighted how in Luke 14 Jesus instructed his followers to enact the hospitality conventions, not in accord with reciprocity conventions but rather in accord with gracious self-giving and self-sacrificial principles. On this showing, the summaries in Acts 2 and 4 reflect the early attempt of the disciples to live up to what Jesus spoke of in Luke 14 about inviting and taking care of the poor and needy.

Thus we should probably conclude the following: (1) Luke, knowing that the initial new act of Jesus at Passover was the breaking of bread, and the phrase "This (bread) is my body" simply identified the ceremony by reference to the initial act rather than calling it the Lord's Supper. The latter phrase may well have had little meaning to a patron and new Gentile convert like Theophilus; (2) the context in which Luke portrays the Lord's Supper as happening in Jerusalem is in a home, not in a synagogue or temple, which is in continuity with the Passover meal; (3) he says literally in Acts 2:42 that they continued faithfully in the teaching of the apostles and in sharing in common, in the breaking of bread and prayer. This sentence is separate from the mention in verse 46 of daily worship in the temple precincts; here it is breaking of bread in homes. This may suggest that the breaking of bread is not connected here to formal worship, which took place in another social locale. But notice that Luke connects the breaking of bread and prayer in 2:42, which is probably another little pointer to the Lord's Supper since the innovative part of Jesus' handling of the Passover is that he took bread, broke it, prayed, and then distributed the bread personally while saying "This (bread) is my body"; (4) the double reference to breaking of bread here in Acts 2 stands in contrast to the absence of such a reference in 4:32-35, the second summary. Perhaps Luke is suggesting that early on the disciples were sharing the Lord's Supper very frequently in homes, perhaps even daily (though properly speaking the word daily refers to worship in the temple in 2:46); (5) notice as well the close connection between the breaking of bread and *koinōnia* in 2:42. In fact, one could take the clause as meaning "in the sharing in common—i.e. the breaking of bread and prayer." If this is correct, then Luke sees the Lord's Supper as a fellowship meal, a meal that has a horizontal dimension binding the disciples to one another and so should be partaken of with great regularity to reinforce that bond. It is interesting, however, that the worship is said to take place in the temple, but the fellowship and sharing in common, in the homes. This suggests a meal context for the early celebration of the Lord's Supper but perhaps not an ordinary early Jewish worship context, for the reference to breaking of bread and prayer can be read to mean the normal things that happened at an early Jewish meal. As is readily apparent, these summaries of Luke are rich though enigmatic, since they are so brief and telegraphic. We wish Luke had told us more.

Such Lukan summaries become especially important when we investigate the earliest full account of the context and nature of the Lord's Supper in 1 Corinthians 11, and we begin to understand why Paul is so irate at the Corinthians for approaching those communal meals and the Lord's Supper that was a part of them as if they were just another highly stratified Greco-Roman style meal where the rich get the rich food and the poor get leftovers or left out.

What happened when the Christian movement went global and started actively recruiting Gentiles, including Gentiles who had no previous contact or connection with the synagogue? What would happen to the in-home fellowship meals and the celebration of the Lord's Supper in that very different ethos and milieu? If Hellenistic customs and ideas about dining had infected and affected the way early Jews celebrated such meals even in the Holy Land, how much more so in places like Corinth? In our next chapter we must look more closely at Greco-Roman dining customs as we work toward examining the chaos in Corinth over meals shared at the homes of big wheels.

Chapter 3

THE TABLE OF THE ENTITLED AND
THE TABLE OF THE LORD

Eating and Drinking in Corinth

Tell them to invite the poor to dinner, take in four or five at a time, not as they do nowadays, though, but in more democratic fashion, all having an equal share, no one stuffing himself with dainties, with the servant standing waiting for him to eat himself to exhaustion . . . only letting us glimpse the platter or the remnant of the cakes. And tell him not to give a whole half of the pig and its head to his master when it is brought in, leaving for the others just the bones. And tell the wine servers not to wait for each of us to ask seven times for a drink, but on one request to pour it out and to hand us at once a big cup, like they do for their master. And let all the guests have the same wine. Where is it laid down that he should get drunk on wine with a fine bouquet while I burst my belly on new stuff?

—Lucian, *Saturnalia*, 21-22

No one smiled at their pretensions when their banners paraded through the streets in homage to a god or emperor. No one found their honorific decrees or their emphatically advertised votes of thanks, even to people miles above

33

them socially, in the least ridiculous. . . . The arrogation of fancy titles raised no laugh against the Sacred Craft of linen-workers, the Most August Center of Wool-Washers, the Most August Union of Fishers. It followed that their internal organization should ape the high-sounding terminology of larger municipal bodies, the nomenclature of officialdom, and honors like . . . the award of gold crowns in their meetings.

—Ramsay MacMullen

WINING AND DINING IN THE FIRST-CENTURY GRECO-ROMAN WORLD

Well before the time of the Roman Empire there was made a distinction between a feast (a *deipna*) and the symposium (from the Greek *symposion*, which literally refers to a group sharing a meal). The latter, at least originally, had started in classical times in Greece and was the ceremony of a closed club or guild. Perhaps originally it was a drinking party amongst close friends or some sort of close-knit group who enjoyed conversation and wine mixed with water. Originally such meals would take place outside and could involve neighbors coming on the spur of the moment, but by the New Testament era it was increasingly common for such a meal to transpire within a home's *triclinium*, or dining room, complete with couches and tables and by invitation only. The Roman era was the era of couch potatoes when it came to dining.

One of the things that changed dining in antiquity was that increasingly, to improve their civic honor rating, city officials would offer a community sacrifice that resulted in large quantities of meat, even beyond the capacity of the elite to consume it all. So on at least some occasions, particularly at religious or Olympic style festivals, the general public would be invited to the cookout (and eat in). In earlier times the communal sacrifice had been undertaken in homes, but before the time of Augustus it had been moved to the temple precincts, which in turn led to the building of considerable dining rooms in those precincts to consume what had been just sacrificed.

This in turn changed the character of the *deipna* or dinner in the home. It became increasingly more like a drinking party or symposium, though some food would be involved as a sort of first course. The Romans called the feast part a *cena* whilst the drinking party that followed they called the *convivia*. What elite persons then did to improve their honor rating with friends and clients was to have combined feasts and drinking parties in the home, basically of a nonreligious character, offered up in two stages: (1) the meal; and then after dismissing the wife and the children, (2) the drinking party (think of men in Victorian England withdrawing to the game room for a smoke, a drink, and perhaps some billiards). To spice up the latter part of the occasion, there would be after-dinner speakers—philosophers or rhetors to entertain the gentlemen when they reclined and drank.[1] In classical Greece the symposion had been more of a serious event, but in Roman times it was seen as more a matter of after-dinner entertainment, hence the term *convivia*, from which we of course get the term *convivial*.

Even a cursory reading of Plutarch's *Lives* will show that drinking parties with disorderly conduct, flaunting of excess and extravagance, treachery and plotting, sexual dalliance with serving girls and others, and general immorality and debauchery were not uncommon. The drinking parties were generally all-male affairs, as the classical club meetings had been earlier. But entertainment might include dancing and flute-playing girls and companions (*hetairai*)—as well as prostitutes at less-refined meals, such as those held by nouveau riche freedmen. Plutarch (*Lyc.* 13.607; *Mor.* 227C) polemicizes against the vulgarity of silver-footed couches, purple coverlets, gold cups and the like in the home of such a freedman. The reason for his ire was that he took behavior at the convivia as a clear indicator of the level of civilized behavior of that person and his household in general. Here we have come across an important, indeed crucial, point—*behavior at meals was taken as an indicator or barometer of the society's or club's or group's character in microcosm.* In other words, what went on at meals most revealed the character of the diners, and was *supposed* to most mirror the values that this particular group upheld. This goes a long way toward explaining why Paul is so upset with the behavior of some high-status Christians at the community meal and celebration of the Lord's Supper (see below).

At the symposium, besides drinking, the chief entertainment was conversation of all sorts about all sorts of subjects including politics, philosophy, religion, economics, and of course gossip and personal matters. Sophists, rhetors, teachers, *and* philosophers were regularly the speakers at such an occasion, and rhetoricians especially might be the guests of honor, since they could offer an encomium on some subject at the drop of a hat and could get the conversation going (cf. Athenaeus, *Deipnosophists*; Philostratus, *Vit. Soph.* 20). It is interesting that such banquets, and the desire to participate in them, were in fact some of the chief inducements getting non-Romans to desire and pursue Romanization. They did not wish to miss out on the party!

The term *convivia* normally referred to smaller dinner parties as opposed to formal public banquets. Christian meals in the home of a member in Corinth would certainly have been seen as this sort of meal, and not surprisingly, partially socialized Gentile Christians in that city would assume that the usual dinner protocols applied. At convivia normally male slaves, called *ministri*, would be the main servers, and they also doubled as doormen and bouncers. The normal protocol was for the more high-status persons, including of course the host, to get the better seats and the better food and drink. The pecking order was so often rigid that one could tell where one stood with the host by how close to the host one was seated, with the guest of honor reclining on the couch with or next to the host. The closer to the host, the more important and honorable you were thought to be. The only exception to this rule tended to be at the once-a-year Saturnalia where masters served slaves and a sort of temporary democracy took place at the meals and in the households (see the quote above). In some respects Christian meals, which involved persons ranging from the elite to slaves, might well have seemed like Saturnalia meals, especially to outsiders.

Who could and did attend the cena and convivia? Normally the host and his wife and occasionally the children would attend the feast, but the wife and children retired before the convivia began. When women did appear or stay for the convivia, they were often assumed to be immoral. It should also be noted that public banquets especially tended to be all-male feasts, especially when the second part of the ceremony began. K. E. Corley summarizes the situation:

> It is clear that women who were associated with banquet settings were seen in the popular imagination as prostitutes. Certain Greco-Roman women did in fact attend dinners with their husbands, but the practice may not have been all that common, even in the associations, and its pervasiveness outside the upper classes is difficult to determine. Areas still influenced by Greek ideals and practices would also still adhere to a certain extent to the exclusion of women from such meals, and certainly from those meals characterized as symposia. Women who did attend such parties would have engendered a great deal of social criticism, particularly after the time of Augustus, when the interest in the maintenance of the nuclear family as a means to insure the political stability of the Empire caused a shift in the social consciousness which reemphasized ideal women's roles. Absence from public banquets became part of that complex of ideas which eventually limited her ability to participate in the public sphere in the centuries to follow.[2]

In the archaeological study of dining rooms (a dining room was called a *triclinium*) in temples in Corinth (e.g. the Asklepion) as well as in private homes, a decided preference is shown for the pattern of having three couches aligned in a C shape facing inward. Each couch in such an arrangement would hold up to three diners, so in a normal dining room, particularly in a home, one might expect twelve to fourteen guests in the triclinium (because the long side of the C could include two couches) while in the temple dining rooms one could seat up to twenty or twenty two. It was possible to have a peristyle garden next to the dining room where slaves and perhaps lesser-status guests could also participate in the family meal or at least wait for the leftovers and take them away. Of course, one could hire a garden-style triclinium and so have an outdoor feast at the local *taberna*, or tavern, and those would be private affairs, whereas a banquet at a temple would tend to be a civic and public affair, though not always. Much of this discussion illuminates texts like 1 Corinthians 10-11, as we shall now see.

THE FULL MEAL DEAL IN CORINTH—1 CORINTHIANS 10

Throughout 1 Corinthians 8-11, which deals with problems involving meals both in temples, in homes, and, in connection with those in-home meals, the celebrating of the Lord's Supper, Paul has several major concerns: (1) he wants to make clear that Christians should not attend feasts or drinking parties in pagan temples at all. The dramatic way he puts it is: "you cannot partake of the table of the Lord and the table of demons" (10:21; (2) Paul does not want his converts to hold their fellowship meals (called *agapais*, or "love-feasts," in Jude 12) according to the rules of Greco-Roman dining, perhaps especially because the Lord's Supper was a part of this larger fellowship meal and occasion. Not surprisingly these strictures came as something of a surprise, a painful one, to more high-status Christians in Corinth who had only partially understood what the practical implications were of being a Christian. Unless we take this latter fact into consideration, namely, that Corinthian Christians were definitely a work in progress, we will not understand what Paul says about meals in general and the Lord's Supper in particular in 1 Corinthians 10-11.

Paul chooses to address his converts in Corinth by using an analogy in the form of a typology in 1 Corinthians 10. The idea behind a typology is that since God's character never changes, God acts in similar ways in different periods of the history of God's people. Furthermore, God provides persons and events that foreshadow other later persons and events in salvation history. Finally, there is also the idea in play that Paul and his converts are living in the eschatological age when "the hopes and fears of all the years are met in thee tonight," to borrow a lyric from a Christmas carol. Paul believes he and his charges are living in the age of fulfillment of all such previous paradigms and prophecies.

Thus, it is no surprise that Paul says to the Corinthians that the things that happen to God's Old Testament people happened, at least in part, as examples to the eschatological people of God and for their benefit, if they will just learn from those examples. Israel then, and the Old Testament in general, provides both negative and positive examples of how Christians should live. In this case, Paul sees a partial analogy between the wicked behavior of some Israelites who had all kinds of benefits from God in the Exodus-Sinai events and in the wilderness wandering period and at least some of the Corinthian Christians. Since God is viewed as still judging such behavior, Paul warns that the outcome for some Corinthian Christians could be as bad as it was for those Israelites. In other words, Paul thinks that apostasy followed by judgment is still as live a possibility in the eschatological age as it was in Old Testament times. Paul wants to know if these persons are willing to sacrifice their salvation for the sake of a piece of meat, much like the story of Esau and his birthright squandered for a bowl of lentel soup. Just as importantly, he wants to know if they are willing to sacrifice the unity of the body of Christ in order to indulge their selfish behavior and preferred social customs. It appears that some of them assumed that because they had participated in the Christian sacraments of baptism and the Lord's Supper, they were guaranteed a happy everlasting life, and of course there are still some Christians who hold such a view. If you know something about ancient religious rituals and ceremonies, you will understand why they might have thought this. While most ancients were looking for immediate benefits from religious rituals (e.g. healing from a ritual performed in the temple of Asklepius, virility or extension of physical life from a bath in the blood of a bull), Plutarch reminds us that many people feel no fear of death, having gone through certain religious initiation rituals, assuming they will assure the person of a blessed afterlife (*Moral.* 1105B). It appears that the Corinthians had some such idea about baptism and perhaps the Lord's Supper. Paul must disabuse them of these notions.

Thus it is that in 1 Corinthians 10 Paul begins by stressing that the Israelites received benefits from the Exodus–Sinai event (the pass through the Red Sea on dry ground is even imaginatively characterized as being baptized into Moses), and they had water and manna miraculously provided for them in the wilderness (presumably the manna and water are seen as types of the Lord's Supper elements). Nevertheless, says Paul, though *all these Israelites* had these spiritual experiences and benefits, yet they perished in the wilderness. To up the rhetorical ante even more, Paul says that the preexistent Christ was the one who provided them with the water from the rock! His point is simply that the Israelites had the same sort of benefits as the Corinthian Christians, and yet participation in those Mosaic "sacraments" did not save them in any way, not even securing them from dying a horrible death in the desert.

Notice that in 1 Corinthians 10:3 Paul calls the manna "spiritual food," by which he presumably means food miraculously provided by God's Spirit, not heavenly tasting or textured food (angel food cake is not in view!). It is not the food or the drink that is spiritual or miraculous; it is simply miraculously provided. Despite all of their benefits God judged most of these Israelites, they died, and their bodies were strewn around in the wilderness. Here Paul is largely answering those who had written him urging that they had a right to go to the dinner parties in pagan temples. Paul must warn them against disastrous spiritual consequences that can follow. It is indeed possible that some Corinthians had a magical view of the Christian sacraments. First Corinthians 1 perhaps suggests this when Paul says in disgust that he is glad he didn't baptize more of the Corinthians, since it led to factional behavior. In the minds of these whom Paul is warning, since they participated in Christian baptism, an initiation rite, and in the Lord's Supper, a communion ceremony, they were spiritually bulletproof. Apparently they assumed that the Christian sacraments delivered at least as much as the pagan ones, and to be sure this might have been an understandable mistake since there was so much talk about salvation and everlasting life as part and parcel of the gospel. A pagan would naturally assume that the spiritual goods were delivered through ritual and ceremony, especially since the heart of pagan religion was the ritual sacrifice, which placated the gods. Paul wants to give a reality check to those who had a false sense of security.

If the Corinthians in question had that false sense of security based on their understanding of the sacraments, they could have reasoned, "What possible spiritual harm can come from going to a dinner party in a pagan temple?" Their mentality is revealed in 1 Corinthians 10:23 where they suggest, "All things are lawful for me" (cf. 1 Cor 6:12). It is precisely such a sense of false security that is seen as dangerous by Paul, and so he must talk about temptations and the need to rely on God's grace to avoid giving in to them. Paul then is suggesting that the Christian sacraments are more like the spiritual benefits Israel had than like the touted benefits of some pagan rituals. Paul says that the Old Testament events serve as a negative example so the Corinthians may avoid spiritual apostasy and self-destruction. Perhaps in order to counter the idea that the Israelites had inferior sacraments to the Christians, Paul stresses that Christ actually provided some of those benefits, thus Paul forestalls one of the possible objections of the Corinthians.

Notice that the longer this argument goes, and it goes on for several chapters, the more it becomes clear that those objecting to Paul's strictures about going to pagan temple feasts are some of the more high-status Gentile Christians who regularly went to such meals and could not see the harm in them. Besides, they would lose face and perhaps lose clients by not going to such meals, since temples were the ancient restaurants of the day for the more well-to-do (the working class would go to taverns or food stands on the streets).

One of the keys to understanding Paul's argument in 1 Corinthians 10 is his use of the term "spiritual" (*pneumatikon*). In what sense was the rock, the food, and the drink spiritual (10:3-4)? Paul is not talking about figurative food and drink, but rather real food and drink; neither is he talking about the character or quality of that real food and drink. The term "spiritual" here has the very same significance it does in 1 Corinthians 15:44. There the contrast is between a natural body and a spiritual body. The contrast has to do with the source of the body. God's Spirit provided the food and drink in the wilderness, and God's Spirit will provide the resurrection body as well. The food, like the body, is a real and material substance, but its origins are different from ordinary food or bodies. A spiritual body, then, means a body given by, and perhaps entirely empowered by, the Spirit. It does not refer to a nonmaterial body. Similarly, spiritual food and drink here refer to real food and drink, but spiritually or miraculously provided.[3] There is then nothing here to suggest that Paul saw the Lord's Supper elements as something magical or "spiritual" in themselves. To the contrary, he is trying to counter magical views of religious rituals and ceremonies.

But why is Paul so against high-status Corinthian Christians' going to pagan temples and dining? In their letter the Corinthians had argued rather cogently that since there are no gods but the one God, where is the harm in going? Paul is, of course, a monotheist, but he does not think pagan deities are simply nothings! His audience had drawn the wrong conclusion from the right doctrine of monotheism. Paul will suggest that, in fact, there are demons involved in pagan religion, and so something spiritual does occur when one goes to a pagan dinner party in the temple. The issue is not menu but venue—and spiritual ethos or context, as we shall see.

Ramsay MacMullen reminds us that religion was

> at the heart of social life, as surely as it must be placed at the heart of cultural activities of every sort. For most people, to have a good time with their friends involved some contact with a god who served as a guest of honor, as master of ceremonies, or as host in the porticoes . . . of his own dwelling. For most people, meat was a thing never eaten and wine to surfeit never drunk save as some religious setting permitted. There existed—it is no exaggeration to say it of all but the fairly rich—no formal social life . . . that was entirely secular. Small wonder, then, that Jews and Christians [held] themselves aloof from anything the gods touched.[4]

Paul did not want his converts to become spiritually polluted, not by pagan food but by food and drink taken in the presence of and in honor of the demonic.

Paul then is exhorting his converts in 1 Corinthians 10 not to be idolaters; he does not object to their eating meat, even non-kosher meat, as is perfectly clear from 1 Corinthians 10:25-27 where he says they may eat any meat that comes from the marketplace (indeed and originally from the temple) and is served in a private home. This meat is not "idol meat" because it is not partaken of in the spiritual and social context where idols and the demons behind them are at large and influencing things. The term *eidolothuton*, which literally means "idol stuff," does not refer to a particular kind or cut of meat, kosher or otherwise; it refers to meat eaten in the presence of and in honor of an idol or demon.[5]

It is worth adding at this juncture that what 1 Corinthians 8-10 is all about is Paul implementing the decree of James as it is found in Acts 15. James there is not forbidding Gentiles from eating certain sorts of foods; he is prohibiting them from going to pagan temples and dining there where those four things—the abominations of idols, blood, things strangled, and sexual immorality, were in play. Basically James, like Paul, wants Gentiles to avoid idolatry and immorality, and one of the best ways to show one is doing that, and so fulfilling the heart of the Ten Commandments, is by staying away from pagan temples where you find such things.

It is not at all accidental that in exhorting the Corinthians in 1 Corinthians 10 not to be idolators Paul cites Exodus 32:6—the story of the golden calf. This text is of special relevance because it involves: (1) an idol, (2) idol worship, (3) idol food, and (4) sexual immorality. This is the perfect parallel to cite if one wants the Corinthians to stay away from what happens in pagan temples, and the reference to sexual immorality in 1 Corinthians 10:8 follows quite naturally here. It is not an accident that everywhere the term "idol stuff" or "idol food" appears in the New Testament, it is always in connection with sexual immorality (cf. here to Acts 15:29 and Rev 2:14, 20). It was not just

Jews who thought there was a spiritual character to meals in pagan temples. Plutarch says, "It is not the abundance of wine or the roasting of meat that makes the joy of festivals, but the good hope and belief that the god is present in his kindness and graciously accepts what is offered" (*Mor.* 1102A). Thus Paul is well within the parameters of plausibility when he tells the Corinthians that when they participate in such temple parties, they are trying to provoke Christ in the same way that the Israelites provoked God at Sinai with the golden calf. Verse 14 is the climax of the first portion of 1 Corinthians 10—"flee from the worship of idols"!

It needs to be said at this point that 1 Corinthians 10:16ff. provides a further argument against idolatry, not, unfortunately, a discourse on the Lord's Supper. Paul only mentions in passing those relevant matters that have to do with the sacrament in order to get the Corinthians to avoid idolatry. Nevertheless, we begin to see some clues here, which we must analyze carefully. At 1 Corinthians 10:16 Paul refers to the "cup of blessing," a technical term for the wine cup drunk at the end of a Jewish meal over which a thanksgiving or grace is said: "Blessed are thou O Lord, who gives us the fruit of the vine." In the Passover meal this was the third of four cups that were to be drunk. This was probably the cup Jesus identified as the cup of the covenant in his blood.[6] The point is that this new covenant is enacted by Christ's death.

As we have already noted, the term *koinōnia* has the sense of sharing or participation in something with someone.[7] It may refer to a worshiper sharing with God something in common, or it may refer to sharing between worshipers, or perhaps in some cases both. The translation of the word as "common participation" gets across the idea that it is a group activity. It is something worshipers do together. What believers are sharing in is not just one another but some third thing to which the word *koinōnia* refers. The translation "fellowship" is not helpful, though fellowship is presumably one of the results of believers sharing or participating in something in common. What then does it mean to share or participate in the blood of Christ together? Apparently Paul thinks more than mere symbols are involved. There seems to be some real, spiritual communion with Christ and others at issue here. Perhaps Paul is thinking of the sharing of the benefits of Christ's death—cleansing, forgiveness, salvation.

Gordon Fee makes the suggestion that the sharing in the cup is vertical (i.e. with Christ) while the sharing in the loaf is horizontal, representing and facilitating believers' sharing with one another as the body of Christ.[8] This requires that the reference to the "body of Christ" in 1 Corinthians 10:16b refer to the body of believers, *not to either* the physical or transcendent body of the individual Christ in heaven *or* some spiritual participation in that ascended-one's body. Comporting with this suggestion is the very next verse, which says, "because there is one bread, we who are many are one body." Paul then is talking about that which binds Christians together into one body of believers. It is not merely the physical sharing in the bread but also the more profound spiritual sharing and uniting that it signifies and facilitates. Another key clue to the meaning of "sharing in common" here is the verb "to partake." The stress on all sharing is because of the coming analogy with Israel in 10:18.

First Corinthians 10:18 explains that the eating of the sacrifice entails a common sharing or participation in the altar. Here we may quote Paul's contemporary Philo: "He to whom sacrifice has been offered makes the group of worshippers partners in the altar and of one table" (using the term *koinōnia—De spec. leg.* 1.221). This in turn suggests that Paul sees the Lord's Supper as a sacrificial meal. What, however, does it really mean to be a participant in the altar? Does it mean sharing in the meat and so the benefits of the sacrifice, or does it actually mean sharing in God as well? Deuteronomy 14:22-27 seems to be in the background here, and so it is unlikely Paul has in mind the notion of actually consuming the deity. In early Judaism, the sacrificial food was never thought of in that way. Thus, probably Paul has in mind sharing in the material and spiritual benefits of Christ's sacrifice. Paul does not mean sharing in Christ's metaphysical being directly or in his glorified flesh. Paul does not see the Lord's Supper as an example of "partaking in the divine nature" (cf. 2 Pet 1:4).

Though idols and idol food are nothing in themselves, Paul nonetheless believes that the demons who use them to entrap humans are something (1 Cor 10:19). One cannot share in God's meal and benefits while at the same time sharing in the demon's meal and the supposed benefits of that. First Corinthians 10:20 says bluntly that Paul does not want them to become common participants with demons by partaking of idol food in a temple. He is speaking of mutually exclusive activities and fellowships here. He, in effect, asks, "Are you just trying to make God angry, or do you think you are stronger than even God, by binding yourself to two antagonistic supernatural sources at once and receiving 'benefits' from both?" Of course the answer to the rhetorical question is no, they are not of such strength or character that they can afford to do such a thing.

In 1 Corinthians 10:30 Paul comes to grips with a possible objection to his ruling: "If I partake with thankfulness, why should I be denounced because of that for which I give thanks?" Paul's answer is clear enough: it's not just a matter of one's own relationship with God; there is also the relationship with fellow believers (especially those weak in faith) to think of and the effects the act may have on them. Verse 31 then states the basic Pauline principle—"Whether you eat or drink, or whatever you do, do everything for the glory of God" and thus also for the edification of one's fellow humans and the building up of the body of Christ. Paul wants his self-centered, high-status Gentile Corinthians to think of others first.

What is interesting about 1 Corinthians 10:32-33 is that it reveals not that Paul is a people pleaser, but that he is happy to be socially accommodating to others so long as the gospel is not compromised. This is a very different posture about food, and especially food not prepared in a kosher way, than he would have had while he was a strict Pharisee before his conversion. In matters of no inherent moral difference such as what one eats or wears, Paul seeks to give no offense to anyone. He is prepared to be all things to all persons so that by all means he may win some. Paul does this not for his own benefit, but in order to save many for Christ. Notice that this section ends with the exhortation "Be imitators of me as I am of Christ" (11:1). This may indeed allude to Jesus' practice of eating with anyone, even notorious sinners, and perhaps to his ruling (see Mark 7) about no food being unclean. It may also refer to Christ's servanthood example, giving up all his rights and privileges for the sake of saving others.

To sum up, Paul in 1 Corinthians 8–10, which is one continuous argument, is exhorting primarily the high-status, "in the know" Gentile Christians who wrote him with questions *and* who have been contending for their freedom to go to pagan feasts and the like in the temples. Paul deliberately defies the expectations of the upwardly mobile and high-status crowd by deconstructing their paradigm and seeking to present meals, and especially the Lord's Supper, in a new light. While he agrees with some of the arguments of the strong, he identifies with the weak, those with too many scruples about meat bought in the market. He wishes to bind together the fractured community in Corinth, and he sees a certain approach to meals and the Lord's Supper as one way to accomplish that aim. But we have not even begun to discuss what Paul actually says in 1 Corinthians 11 about the Lord's Supper itself. To that we must now turn.

GUESS WHO'S COMING TO DINNER? THE LORD HIMSELF— 1 CORINTHIANS 11

Certainly one of the most disputed texts in a letter full of disputed texts is 1 Corinthians 11:17-34. We can only hope to attend to the details relevant to our understanding of the early practice of the Lord's Supper in Corinth. Even so, there is much to say. First we must bear in mind the context. Beginning at 1 Corinthians 11:2 Paul is dealing with abuses in Christian worship, a discussion that will continue until the end of 1 Corinthians 14. Since he is correcting problems of various sorts throughout, unfortunately he does not provide us with a positive exposition of his view of the Lord's Supper. Nevertheless, there is a lot to be learned from this passage, not least of which is how the ceremony was being practiced in the mid-first century in Corinth. It appears clear from the outset that the context in which the Lord's Supper happened was in a home and in the social setting of a meal, perhaps a love feast that was part of an act of worship in the home. The problem was, some of the Christians, perhaps including the host who would set the protocol for the meal, were treating the meal as if it were a private Greco-Roman dinner party followed by a drinking party. The result of this approach, (which Paul sees as a travesty and sacrilege, a violation of the very meaning of Christian fellowship and the meaning of the Lord's Supper), is that there is further stratification and division amongst the have and have-not portions of the Corinthian church. This selfish behavior further threatened the fragile unity of this small Christian community.

Paul is talking about behavior we would call inappropriate "in church," but since the church met in a house, he will say that it is also inappropriate "in house" or at least in a Christian house. The overlap between house and church settings led, no doubt, to some social confusion as to what the conventions of behavior should be. E. A. Judge reminds us of "the talkative, passionate, and sometimes quarrelsome circles that met to read Paul's letters over their evening meal in private houses."[9] I am not so sure, however, that it was simply the ordinary evening meal we are talking about. Ordinary evening meals surely did not regularly include the Lord's Supper. We must think of something even more reprehensible. The meeting was not just a reading circle of Christians, but a regular worship meeting when they all came together. The meal taken in the context of that meeting was a love feast, or a specifically Christian one shared by the body meeting in that house. Within the context of that meal the Lord's Supper was taken. And yet somehow, someway, there were those who treated even this meal in that specific religious context as if it were another Greco-Roman dinner party. This I would suggest explains the very strong response and rhetoric of Paul in 1 Corinthians 11:17-34.

Paul, from the outset, is upset with two facets of what is happening—the disorderliness of the proceedings, which even carries over into the time of sharing spiritual gifts (see 1 Cor 14) and the inequality of the proceedings. It is especially the latter that comes to the fore by the end of the passage. Neither of these problems, however, were at all uncommon in Greco-Roman meals, especially at the drinking-party portion of the event.

One of the things that becomes clear as one works through 1 Corinthians 11:17-34 is that Paul expects the meal Christians share to be far more egalitarian in nature than a normal Greco-Roman meal. He is trying to construct a social practice that would, in fact, go against the flow of the culture's norms in several respects, not the least of which is that he wants all, from the lowest to the highest status, to wait for one another and partake together. Paul's strategy, as Stephen Barton has pointed out, is to make a distinction between private meals in one's own home, and a meal shared in and by the "assembly of God," the *ekklēsia* as Paul calls it.[10] Here is another telltale piece of evidence that it is a clear mistake to assume that Paul simply applied the patriarchal and stratified structure of the household and its conventions to the community of faith. Even though the community meets in the household of one of the more socially well-off Christians, Paul insists that they carry on in a way that comports with the equality that exists in the body of Christ, without regard to social distinctions and social status. The meeting does not involve a matter of sacred space or sacred buildings but rather sacred time, occasion, and events. Paul does not talk about holy buildings, but rather holy persons and holy actions of worship and fellowship. These occasions are to be regulated by sacred traditions, in this case the narrative of the Last Supper provides certain norms. The Lord's Supper is seen as a sacrament or ceremony of communion, both vertical and horizontal in character. It is clearly not seen as a rite of incorporation.

But it is not just that Paul must swim against the tide of household protocol and society's rules when it comes to meetings and meals in

Christian homes. Since early Christians had no purpose-built build-ings, indeed no temples, priests, or physical sacrifices, it is likely that they would have been viewed by many as followers of some sort of philosophy, or like an association, a guild, or a *collegium*, and that their meetings might well be expected by some Corinthians to conform to the way such association meetings went. There are various ways in which a Christian meeting might look like an ancient association meeting. For one thing, both involved people up and down the social scale. Both could include a wealthy patron who was the host, a group of artisans both free and freed, and even some slaves. We know, for example, that there was a trade association of leatherworkers.[11] We also know that a collegium might well meet in homes for a dinner, though normally they would meet in a temple or in their own clubhouse (cf. CIL 9.148 for a dinner in the home of one Sergiae Paullinae). The trade association of leatherworkers is of relevance to our discussion of the Corinthian church because Acts 18 informs us that Paul, Priscilla, and Aquila all practiced this trade; indeed it seems the trade is what brought them together in Corinth. Since Paul was seen to practice this trade in Corinth, from the outset his circle might well have been thought of as an association involving members of that trade and other friends. Sometimes trade associations may have been set up to protect a group of people who also practiced a suspect religion, one that Rome would view as a *superstitio*. The association meetings could involve vari-ous religious activities and functions that, within the context of the association, would not be banned by the local officials since the asso-ciation and trade was a normal and accepted one. One of the main functions of such associations was to provide a vehicle for those who had social aspirations. They were given a venue in which they could be appreciated and gain honor and acclaim from their peers.

One of the more striking correspondences between what we find in 1 Corinthians and these associations comes to light when we con-sider the rules of these associations. Dennis Smith summarizes some of the more common rules:

(1) Injunctions against quarreling and fighting, (2) injunctions against taking the assigned place of another, (3) injunctions against speaking out of turn or without permission, (4) injunctions against fomenting factions, (5) injunctions against accusing a fellow member before a public court, (6) specifications for trials within the club for intraclub disputes, (7) specifications for worship activities.[12]

We may cite a specific example of the guild of Zeus Hypsistos, a religious association of the first century B.C. that had rules against factions, chattering, and indicting one another.[13] What is stunning about all this is that every single one of the listed concerns is addressed by Paul in one way or another in 1 Corinthians. Paul at least seems to be viewing the Corinthian assembly as like some of the more egalitarian associations, or at least implying it should be more like them. Smith goes on to argue that 1 Corinthians 11–14 describes first a meal, then a drinking party, followed by religious activities that took place thereafter, as described in 1 Corinthians 12–14. This would follow the normal pattern of events in a religious association.[14] This might explain some of the chaos addressed in 1 Corinthians 14—some of the participants may have been inebriated, indeed some may have even seen inebriation as the means to set aside one's inhibitions and allow the Spirit to speak through them.

There was normally a transition from the meal to the drinking party, and in the case of a pagan meeting it would involve a libation, a pouring out of a cup of wine to the patron deity, and then singing a hymn to the god (see Plato, *Sympos.* 176A; Athenaeus, *Deiphnos* 15.675b-c). Smith suggests that the Christians replaced the transition with the celebration of the Lord's Supper, which ended with the cup being shared and a hymn being sung. This may well be correct. The drinking party would then continue, and the after-dinner speech or dialogue or teaching would ensue. Plutarch says that the subject matter of the symposium could well be lessons on piety or exhortations to charitable acts and the like (*Quest. Conviv.* 697E).

As we have already noted, meals were an occasion for either gaining or displaying one's social status, as they were microcosms of the competitive nature and values of the culture as a whole. Paul's attempt to deconstruct some of this socially stratifying and individualistic behavior as it was happening at the Lord's meal goes directly against what many would have seen as the real function of such meals—an attempt to show off, strut one's stuff (including one's bling-bling). The ekklesia was, of course, not exactly identical with the associations, nor was it intended to be, as Wayne Meeks points out:

> The Christian groups were exclusive and totalistic in a way that no club nor even the pagan cultic association was. . . . To be "baptized into Christ Jesus" nevertheless signaled for Pauline converts an extraordinarily thoroughgoing resocialization, in which the sect was intended to become virtually the primary group for its members, supplanting all other loyalties. The only convincing parallel in antiquity was conversion to Judaism. . . . Students of private associations generally agree that their primary goals were fellowship and conviviality. . . . The goals of the Christians were less segmented; they had to do with "salvation" in a comprehensive sense. . . . The Christian groups were much more inclusive in terms of social stratification and other social categories than were the voluntary associations.[15]

Meeks however goes on to point out the similarities between Christian meetings and association meetings. Both groups were small, involved intense face-to-face interactions, with membership being decided by voluntary association, not by birth, although of course trade associations presupposed a particular trade. My point is not that Christian assemblies were association meetings but that they were similar enough that some Corinthians would have viewed their meeting as like a religious-association meeting, and so behaving accordingly. Paul is aware of this and is countering certain tendencies in that direction. For him, the function of reciting the sacred tale about the night when Jesus was betrayed was to encourage unitive behavior and social leveling, thus overcoming factionalism and creating harmony in the congregation.

Notice that the discussion that begins at 1 Corinthians 11:17-18 immediately mentions divisions happening when the Corinthians gather in the home for worship. The division is between the haves and have-nots, such that some are going hungry at the meal while others are gorging themselves and getting drunk. It appears once more that the real troublemakers for Paul were the high-status Gentile Christians, or social climbers, who were following the social customs of the larger culture and perhaps of association meetings when it came to meetings with meals. There are several ways to envision what was going wrong. The text may imply that the well-to-do were going ahead and eating without the poor who were arriving late after work, thus going without their fair share. This view depends on translating *ekdexesthe* as "wait for one another" in verse 33, which is certainly possible. Perhaps more likely is the suggestion that the well-to-do are eating in the triclinium while the others were eating in the atrium or peristyle garden, and further that there were two sorts of foods being served to the two groups. The verb in verse 33 can often have the sense of "welcome" one another or even "entertain" one another when it is used in the context of a meal (cf. 3 Macc 5:26; Josephus, *Ant.* 7.351). In any case whether the problem was timing or location, the result was divisions in the body between the haves and have-nots. Paul says he half-believes the reports about this behavior, not because he doubts it, but because it is seen as such a violation of Christian behavior that it was scarcely imaginable.

First Corinthians 11:20 mentions coming together in one place. Apparently there were enough Corinthian Christians that they did not always do this. But what is crucial for our purposes is that Paul implies that the reason for the bigger meeting is the partaking of the Lord's meal. This was something the whole body was to do together. Here we may think back to Acts 2:43-47, which suggests they all met together in one place, were of one accord, and all partook of the Christian meal together. Paul knows of the paradigm, and the Corinthians were far from emulating the model. Clearly enough, in Corinth the Lord's Supper was a part of a larger meal and meeting, something Acts 2 also suggests. Since Paul says some are drunk at the Lord's meal, we must imagine that the Lord's Supper was taking place after the normal meal, perhaps even after the drinking party as well, though the text is not clear on this point. It would appear that the Lord's Supper was not viewed as, or had not at this juncture been transformed into, a ritualistic act that was part of a worship act distinguishable from a fellowship meal. On the contrary, meals, the Lord's Supper, and worship were all part of one ongoing event. The implications of this for current practice will be discussed in due course.

What shall we say about 1 Corinthians 11:21? Paul can hardly mean each has his or her own meal, brought individually to the meeting, for clearly some are going without. What he likely means is that the more well-to-do he is particularly critiquing have their own meals. Much depends on how we take the word *prolambanei* here. Does it mean "to go beforehand" or to "anticipate," in which case the haves were eating before the others? Or does it simply mean "to take" coupled with "to eat"? The lexical evidence slightly favors the former reading. But even so, then the point may not be about late-arriving poor folks, but rather that the wealthy are being served first and getting the better portions, while the poor in the atrium get the leftovers. In any case, the end result is that one is gorged and drunk and another goes hungry. This hardly amounts to a shared common meal. The problems that Paul deals with in 1 Corinthians primarily have to do with things that work against the unity of the group. The goal of Paul's rhetoric here is to remove obstacles to that unity.

In one sense, knowing even a little about human nature, we can easily understand how this problem arose. The host was reasonably well-to-do, and so quite naturally he invited his friends to dine with him in the dining room, whilst the socially less elite were left to fend for themselves in the atrium or garden. The result was further stratification of an already divided group of people.

First Corinthians 11:22a makes very plain that the problem is the well-to-do who have houses enough in which to have their own dinner parties. Notice that Paul does not rule out such sumptuous feasts. His point is that pagan rules of dining protocols absolutely have no place in a Christian-meal situation, much less in a Christian meeting and dinner that also involves the Lord's Supper. The better-off Christians are showing no respect for the have-nots, but even worse, they are not showing the proper respect for the Lord and his meal. The meal itself is being violated, not just general fellowship or even the ekklesia in general.

It is not surprising, then, that Paul's way of correcting the problems is reminding the Corinthians of the traditions he and they share about the Lord's Supper. In 1 Corinthians 11:23 he uses the semitechnical language of Judaism for the passing on of sacred traditions. Here is where we note that this text suggests there was a deliberate passing on of this story in a rather set form, and now it has made its way to Corinth. But Paul is not mentioning this for the first time here. This is tradition Paul had already passed along to the Christians in Corinth. Indeed, it seems to have been one of the first things he handed on to them, presumably in order to set up the practice of the Lord's Supper meal from the outset of the community. This is a tradition Paul received, and we must take this to mean from the Jerusalem community itself, perhaps even from someone like Peter, who was hiself present at the Last Supper (see Gal 1–2). Paul presumably does not mean literally that it was Jesus who handed him this tradition, but that it goes back to Jesus himself ultimately. That this was a tradition mediated to Paul by other Christians is shown by the closeness of the Pauline form of the tradition of the words and story to the Lukan form, and its differences from the Markan and Matthean forms of the story and words. I would prefer to say that the Lukan form reflects the Pauline form, rather than the converse, since Luke wrote at a later time and after being Paul's sometime companion over the years. The important point is this: Paul's record is chronologically the earliest we have of this crucial material. Unfortunately, he only selectively quotes his source as he is busy correcting abuses and problems, not making a positive exposition of things.

First Corinthians 11:23 makes clear that the Lord's Supper was a tradition involving a historical memory of an actual event. It is thus set off from pagan memorial meals of various sorts. One of the regular features of the latter sort of meal was that the person about to die would leave in his will a stipend and stipulation that there be a memorial feast in his honor. Diogenes Laertius, for example, records that Epicurus left provision for an annual celebration "in memory of us" (10.16-22). The Corinthians may well have seen the Lord's Supper as a funerary memorial meal. One of the main differences of course would be that in the Lord's Supper one does not merely celebrate the life of the deceased Jesus; one communes with the living Christ, and one also proclaims his death until he comes again, by having this meal and by other means. The pagan funerary meals were often taken on the graves of the deceased, because it was believed that while they were in Hades, they were still alive and could partake of the meal with the living in some sense. Archaeologists have in fact found pouring spouts going down into the grave so wine could be poured into it! The Lord's Supper stands out from Passover as well in that the Lord's Supper celebrates a historical person and his deeds, whereas Passover celebrates the divine actions of Yahweh in the Exodus-Sinai events. There were salient differences between these three sorts of memorial meals.

The reference to Jesus' betrayal or being handed over (*paredideto* can mean either in 1 Cor 11:23) marks off the Lord's Supper from all pagan celebrations that focused on myths. There is a poignancy to this beginning of the ceremony as it reminds us that one of Jesus' own disciples betrayed him, and this in the context of a meal meant at least to bind the disciples closer to Jesus and to indicate the forgiveness they had from him. If we look carefully at this text, the following points come to light: (1) there is no association here of the breaking of the bread with the breaking of Jesus' body, despite the later textual variants that tried to slant the tradition in this direction. Nothing at all is suggested about reenacting the Passion in this ceremony. The breaking of the bread would not be a reenactment anyway since no bone of Jesus' body was broken; (2) notice the double reference to "for my memory/memorial" or "in remembrance of me" after both the bread and the cup words. This may be Paul's own emphasis here, since only

Luke and Paul have the memory clauses; (3) only Paul says they are to celebrate the Lord's Supper as often as they drink of the wine cup. Not all meals involved wine. For the poor especially this would be for special occasions; (4) in the Last Supper meal the language was clearly figurative, as we have seen, following the lead of the symbolic use of language in the Passover.[16] This had to be the case, since Jesus was not yet dead; indeed he was physically present with them at that meal. Jesus seems to have been modifying elements in the Passover meal and referring them to himself. This must count against any sort of overly literal interpretation of the "words of institution"; (5) the phrase *hyper humōn* ("that is for you") is found only in the Pauline/Lukan form of the tradition (1 Cor 11:24; Luke 22:19-20). It probably alludes to Isaiah 53:12 indicating that Christ gave his body on the believers' behalf and/or in the believers' place. The breaking of the bread is associated with and reminds us of that act of self-giving of his body and life; (6) what Jesus did at the Last Supper should not be seen as a funerary rite. This is not Jesus' last will and testimony, for the word *new* here, referring to a new covenant or testament, is fatal to such a view. The term *diatheke* or "covenant" should be seen as a reference to the founding of a new covenant relationship through the shedding of Jesus' blood. Thus the remembering here is not merely a matter of a yearly memorial service for Jesus, like the pagan funerary meals. Indeed, the mention of having this meal whenever all the Corinthians come together suggests a frequent occasion, a regular ceremony involving something more positive than just a funerary remembrance rite. The ceremony of the Lord's Supper is a visible Word proclaiming the dead-but-risen Jesus until he comes and what he has done for them in his death and resurrection; (7) Jesus is said to have broken the bread only after giving thanks. This does not prove he was celebrating a Passover meal, since the giving of thanks was part of any Jewish meal. Nevertheless, the other features of this historical memory certainly suggest he was celebrating a Passover meal; (8) the reference to the wine cup coupled with the reference to some getting drunk makes perfectly clear that the early celebration of the Lord's Supper did involve wine with some alcoholic content; it was not mere grape juice; (9) notice that Paul does not specifically link the cup to Jesus' blood. It is rather called the cup of the new covenant, which is "in my blood" (i.e., instituted by the death of Jesus). It is certainly beyond either Jesus' or Paul's meaning to suggest that the audience was being asked to drink Jesus' blood, something Jews would react to in horror, as would pagans. Paul says nothing about the wine being or representing Christ's blood. That is found in the Markan tradition; (10) Paul stresses that the meal involves both eating and drinking, but it also includes the words said—proclaiming Christ's death, until he returns. Thus the meal has past, present, and future orientations. It does not just focus on the past. One may suspect that the Aramaic cry *maran atha* (cf. 1 Cor 16:22), "Our Lord, come!" was an integral part of the original celebration of the Lord's Supper by the earliest Jewish Christians. The Lord's Supper then is an essential witness to the crucified, risen, and returning Lord. The Lord's coming mentioned here prepares for the discussion about coming judgment in the following verses.

The reference in 1 Corinthians 11:27 is to Christ's actual body, which was crucified, as the reference to blood makes evident. *Anaziōs* has been translated "in an unworthy manner," and sometimes incorrectly thought to modify not the way of partaking but the character of the persons partaking. But Paul refers to those who are partaking in an unworthy manner, not those who in themselves as unworthy, which presumably Paul would see as including any and all believers. No one is worthy of partaking of the Lord's Supper; it's not a matter of personal worth. Paul is rather concerned with the abuse in the actions of the participants, or at least some of them. Paul says that those who partake in an unworthy manner, abusing the privilege, are liable or guilty in some sense of the body and blood of Jesus. They are, in addition, partaking without discerning or distinguishing "the body."

Perhaps Paul means such abusers are guilty of standing on the side of those who abused and even killed Christ—an atrocious sacrilege. Perhaps, like the author of Hebrews (see Heb 6) he is indirectly accusing them of crucifying Christ afresh. The concept of sacrilege was widespread in Paul's era. For example, Dionysius of Halicarnassus says, "those who try to abolish a custom were regarded as having done a thing deserving both the indignation of human beings and the vengeance of the gods . . . a justifiable retribution by which the perpetrators were reduced from the greatest height of glory they once enjoyed to the lowest depths" (*Rom. Ant.* 8.80.2). Paul is saying something similar to this about those who have become sick and died. Those Corinthians had partaken of the Lord's Supper in an unworthy manner and had been judged by God for doing so. Paul uses this as a solemn warning to the other Corinthians against continuing to abuse the Christian meal.

It is crucial to recognize that juridical language permeates this entire section of the discourse. We have, for example, the use of *enoxos* (guilty/liable, v. 27), *dokimazetō* (examine, 11:28), *krima* (judgment), *diakrinōn* (distinguishing, recognizing, v. 29), *ekrinometha* (be judged, v. 31), *katakrinōmen* (condemned, v. 32). The examination referred to in verse 28 means that one must reflect on how one is partaking of the meal; it is not about introspection to determine if one is worthy. Notice that when Paul refers to discerning "the body" (v. 29) it is only "the body" not the "body and blood" or even "the Lord" that is to be discerned in the partaking of the meal. While this might be a reference to remembering Christ's death when one eats, it seems more likely in this larger context to refer to the body of believers. One is to be cognizant that this is a group meal, a group-building ceremony. The least probable interpretation is that Paul is warning against forgetting the sacramental presence of Christ in the elements. The Corinthians are eating in a selfish and self-centered manner without taking cognizance of their brothers and sisters present. They should be partaking with them as one body of Christ, rather than following pagan protocol that gives the elite better treatment and first dibs on the meal.

Paul believes that the Corinthians are bringing judgment on themselves, both temporally in the form of weaknesses and illnesses, and possibly even permanently in eternal condemnation. Paul even says that because of this very failure "some have died" (11:30), a shocking conclusion. Paul must have believed he had some prophetic insight into the situation, which we at so great a remove do not have. It is presumably not the food that made them ill, but the judgment that came upon them for partaking in an unworthy manner. Such disasters can be avoided, says Paul, if the Corinthians will simply examine themselves and their behavior and remember their fellow believers who are their equals in Christ before they partake (11:31). Perhaps Paul sees the judgment of illness a temporal judgment meant to prevent a worse disaster of being condemned with the world of nonbelievers at the Last Judgment when Christ returns. If this is correct, Paul may view the illness as corrective or remedial rather than some sort of final judgment on a person.

First Corinthians 11:33 then provides a final word of remedial advice. The verb *ekdesesthe*, while it may mean "wait for one another," is perhaps more likely in this context to mean welcome one another, show gracious hospitality to one another, partake together with one another without distinctions in rank and food. The point of the Lord's meal is something other than satisfying hunger, or at least this is not the main point. Thus the meal must not be treated as just another banquet. First Corinthians 11:34 lets us know that Paul had plenty more to say about these matters, but it would have to wait until he was present with the audience. This verse makes so very clear the ad hoc nature of this whole discussion. It is not a preconceived treatise on the Lord's Supper; it is rather pastoral remarks by a minister trying to correct abuses in the way the Supper was being taken.

AND SO?

What have we learned in our examination of Paul's discussion of meals, and in particular the Lord's Supper? Firstly, the Lord's Supper was taken in homes. This is clear not only from 1 Corinthians 11 but also probably from Acts 2, and furthermore, it was partaken of as a part of a larger fellowship meal. Secondly, Paul is trying to distinguish the Christian meal and its protocol from the usual socially stratifying customs of a pagan meal. The Christian meal was to depict the radical leveling that the kerygma proclaimed—whoever would lead must take on the role of the servant, and all should be served equally. This social leveling was meant to make clear that there was true equality in the body of Christ. All were equal in the eyes of the Lord, and they should also be viewed that way by Christians, leading to equal hospitality toward all.

Thirdly, the Lord's Supper was clearly not just a reenactment of the Passover meal, not least because of its prospective element, looking forward and pointing forward to the return of Christ. For that matter, the Last Supper itself was no ordinary Passover meal, for Christ modified both the elements and their interpretation so they would refer to him and his coming death. There seems to be no historical evidence that early Christians used the Lord's Supper as an occasion to dramatize either the Passover or the Last Supper. Instead, the ceremony was incorporated into a larger and different context, that of the Christian fellowship, or agape, meal. Christ himself was viewed as the Christians' Passover through his death and its benefits. What Paul says in 1 Corinthians 5:7-8 is telling: "Christ, our Passover Lamb, has been sacrificed for us. So let us celebrate the festival, not by eating the old bread of wickedness and evil, but by eating the new bread of purity and truth" (NLT). The death of Christ, if rightly understood, not merely supercedes the old Passover, but is meant to change the pattern of the ways God's people behave. Notice that Paul refers to eating bread here as an allusion to the Christian meal, just as we saw in Acts 2.

While nothing in the Pauline discussion of the Lord's Supper suggests that the meal was seen as a foreshadowing of the messianic banquet, it appears likely that Jesus himself saw the Last Supper that way (Mark 14:25). Thus the idea of the Lord's Supper pointing forward to the messianic banquet is appropriate even if neither Paul nor Luke suggest it.

We must note that surely it was the fact that the Lord's Supper was being partaken of in homes that led to the assumptions that this was just another celebratory meal, which in turn led to the abuses Paul is trying to correct.

One of the most important conclusions one can draw from a close reading of 1 Corinthians 10–11 is that Paul does not assume that the Lord's Supper is a purely symbolic meal. He believes there is a spiritual transaction going on in this meal just as there was in the meal at the pagan temple. The right sort of spiritual communion between Christ and his people can be contrasted with the wrong sort of spiritual communion between demons and their worshipers. In short, Paul was no Zwinglian, but as it turns out, even Zwingli was not an advocate of a purely symbolic interpretation of the Lord's Supper.[17]

There is more to be said about these matters, but we will leave that for subsequent chapters. What we must do now is turn to John 13–17 and evaluate whether any light is shed on the Lord's Supper discussion by this very different material, or whether, in fact, those chapters describe a different meal altogether.

Chapter 4

THE LONG FAREWELL

The Feast in John 13–17

"You received me," he says, "into your home. I will receive you into the King-
dom of my Father; you took away my hunger, I take away your sins . . . you
saw me a stranger, I make you a citizen of heaven; you gave me bread, I give
thee an entire Kingdom, that you may inherit and possess it."

—John Chrysostom (*Homily 45 on Acts*)

Scholars have long had difficulty assessing various features of the Farewell Discourse found in John 13–17, precisely because these chapters
seem so very different from the Synoptic accounts of the Last Supper.[1]

FRAMEWORK FOR A FEAST

It is apparent to most that there is no evidence in John 13–17 at all
that Jesus is celebrating a Passover meal. Instead we are told at the
outset that not only did this event occur before the day of the Passover,
it occurred "before the [entire] festival of the Passover" (13:1). The
speculation of the disciples about Judas going and buying supplies for

the Passover in 13:29 surely also comports with the conclusion that John 13 at least is referring to events including a meal that transpired prior to Passover. Furthermore, John 13:1 must be compared to John 12:1, which has the phrase "six days before the [festival of] Passover." The overall impression left by the sequence of John 12–13 is that the meal described in John 13 occurred sometime during the week of Unleavened Bread/Passover celebration but not necessarily on the eve of Passover.

A second and important observation is that scholars of all stripes, including many conservative ones, have recognized that the "discourse" in John 13:31–17:26 are discourses, plural, and do not represent things said on just one occasion. They have been combined here to indicate the sort of in-house teaching Jesus offered his disciples at the end of his ministry. Certainly John 14:31 indicates that the discourse is over, and in fact the natural sequel to 14:31 is John 18:1. I would suggest then that this teaching was offered on successive nights of Passover week leading up to Good Friday, and the Fourth Evangelist has put the material into his own idiom and combined it to give the gist or pith of the teaching. Clear enough from 13:21-30, our author includes some Last Supper traditions as well as some other material, but in fact he *nowhere narrates an account of the Last Supper Passover and Jesus' reorientation of it.* We need to ask why our author has put this material together the way he has, and what is the significance of it? Is it really the case that John 13:1-30 is only loosely connected to what follows it?

Here is the basic framework I am operating with for interpreting this material, after close study of these chapters. Firstly, the Fourth Evangelist is portraying the disciples' sharing a farewell dinner, which was actually a series of dinners, with Jesus. Secondly, the dinner is not portrayed as a Passover meal, which is shown not only by the time reference in 13:1 but also by the lack of any interpretation of the Passover elements in any of these chapters. Ironically the closest we get is in connection with the Galilean feeding miracle in John 6:53-56, not in connection with the last week of Jesus' life and his impending death. Our author's concern there however is not with the consuming of sacramental elements but with the taking of Christ into one's life so that one may have eternal life. He does not make a connection between the latter and either the Passover meal or the Last Supper. In any case, it is well to bear in mind, as Fred Craddock says, that in the Fourth Gospel "Jesus does not eat the Passover, he is the Passover."[2]

Instead of a Passover meal, we have a portrayal of a Greco-Roman banquet complete with closing symposion and the religious rites associated with such a meal. Jesus acts here as the sage, philosopher, and rhetor and offers his after-dinner teaching. Note that this practice was common from the highest eschalons of society right down to ordinary meals with ordinary participants. The emperor Nero's regular practice was to call in the teachers of "wisdom" after dinner to amuse the guests.[3] Jesus, by contrast, is portrayed in the Fourth Gospel as God's wisdom come in the flesh, and his discourse will not provide entertainment but rather spiritual enlightenment.

This is not unlike what we find in 1 Corinthians 11–14, where Paul describes a worship event that involves a meal, a symposion, and closing religious acts. In order to see this connection and the Johannine presentation properly, a few further remarks about the Jewish celebration of such Hellenistic meals is needed. We noted in the last chapter that Paul was using the Lord's Supper as a theological tool to deconstruct the stratification of society usually encapsulated in meals. Here we note that Jesus, by the footwashing episode at the meal, coupled with his prayer for unity in John 17, is depicted as undertaking the same kind of social rearrangement of perceptions and practices. Jesus will have experienced on various occasions the nature of such Hellenistic-styled meals modified to Jewish tastes, as the description of the meal at the house of Simon the Pharisee in Luke 7:36-50 makes quite clear. Notice at verses 44-45 Jesus expects footwashing to be a regular service a hospitable host would provide for a guest at such a meal. He missed this service when Simon did not provide it. Notice as well that in Luke 22:24-27 in the context of the Last Supper there is a discussion of who is the greatest, followed by a deconstruction of such talk by Jesus with his providing a pattern of servant leadership as in John 13.

One of the crucial and distinguishing features of John 13–17 is that Jesus was partaking of a Greco-Roman-style meal, for we are told at 13:23-25 that the Beloved Disciple was reclining next to Jesus. This suggests that either the Beloved Disciple is the host or chief guest at this meal, but in any case Jesus takes on the responsibility of the host and the job of the host's servant by undertaking to wash his disciples' feet. Normally this would be the task of the household slave. The act is portrayed as a typical Johannine prophetic-sign act, but the point is reinforced because it was a regular part of hospitality at the Jewish celebration of a Greco-Roman meal, not least in Israel because of the arid climate and many unpaved roads. Here this opening act, coupled with the closing prayer, serves the purpose of creating unity among the inner group of disciples, especially in view of the coming betrayal, denial, and general desertion of the Twelve.

The mention of the common purse in John 13:28-30 is reminiscent of meals held by associations and *collegia*. There would be a treasurer's report, and charitable acts and future spending would be discussed (cf. Luke 22:35-38 and John 12 and the protest about the extravagance of the anointing).

A good deal of the material in John 13–17 falls into the category of a farewell discourse or dialogue. But this is done in the context of a meal such that Jesus is presented here as the sage or philosopher who is offering those reclining at the table some reflections. John 13:31–16:33, which contains these addresses, is an especially appropriate sequel to John 13:1-30 seen in the light of Greco-Roman meal conventions.

The so-called high priestly prayer in John 17 was an appropriate closing act at the end of the discourse that followed the meal. As we noted in the last chapter, the religious acts usually came at the end of the convivia. We may compare the sage's concluding prayer in Sirach 51. The character of the prayer in John 17 suggests divisions and that some have gone out and betrayed the Christ, like Judas. As addressed to the audience of the Beloved Disciple at the end of the first century, this material would be of relevance for dealing with factionalism (see 2

John 7–11). What is interesting is that both here and in 1 Corinthians 11, speech at and about the meal is used to produce unity and harmony among the disciples.

John 16:25-27 makes evident that Jesus is not presented as just any sort of sage or wise man but as a Jewish sage who speaks parabolically and explains his figures of speech to his disciples in this setting. What is happening here is that Jesus is being portrayed as God's Wisdom come in the flesh, like Wisdom in Proverbs 8-9 who built her house and then called her disciples to a feast, even the immature and simple ones, invoking them with the words "Come, eat of my bread and drink of the wine . . . live, and walk in the way of insight" (Prov 9:5-6). Once more before his return to the Father, Jesus calls his disciples to hear and heed the voice of Wisdom, but he does so knowing that rejection will follow. First Enoch 42 is especially relevant here as it depicts Wisdom rejected by God's people and returning on high to be with God. The disciples here are portrayed just like the "simple" of Proverbs for they do not understand a whole host of things, including what is going on between Jesus and his betrayer (John 13:28-29), nor do they grasp what is the "way" that both Jesus and Wisdom in Proverbs 9 spoke of.

If we ask for the reason why this whole complex of material is portrayed as like what happens at a Greco-Roman meal rather than a Passover meal, the answer is that this material is now part of a missionary document addressed to Jewish Christians in Asia Minor.[4] While Jesus is portrayed as a Jewish sage and Wisdom, the portrayal highlights the more universal aspects of his character and teaching (cf. e.g. John 1), which would work well with Hellenized Jewish Christians in the Diaspora. In other words, Jesus is portrayed as offering teaching that anyone in the Greco-Roman world could make sense of and relate to.

These chapters conclude with words and allusions to the ongoing missionary work of the disciples (cf. 15:16; 17:21, 33). In short, these chapters are not so much written *about* the Johannine community of the Beloved Disciple and its communal history and development; they are now edited together to encourage that community to continue their missionary work in spite of pressure and resistance and false teachers. They are to continue to evangelize when they enter synagogues and other places to witness (15:18-20; 16:1; 17:4) even though they face persecution and expulsion and even though there may be divisions in the community itself (see 2 and 3 John). The above provides a general orientation of how these chapters are meant to be heard and read in light of their sapiential character. But we need to add another component to our discussion at this juncture—who was this person that reclined with Jesus at this meal, and does this help us to understand better what is going on in John 13–17?

THE HISTORICAL FIGURE OF THE BELOVED DISCIPLE IN THE FOURTH GOSPEL

Martin Hengel and Graham Stanton, among other scholars, have reminded us in recent discussions of the Fourth Gospel that the superscripts to all four of the canonical Gospels were in all likelihood added after the fact to the documents; indeed they may originally have been added as document tags to the papyrus rolls. Even more tellingly, they were likely added only after there were several familiar gospel accounts, for the phrase "according to . . ." is used to distinguish this particular gospel from other well-known ones.

This means, of course, that all four gospels are formally anonymous and the question then becomes how much weight one should place on internal evidence of authorship (the so-called inscribed author) and how much on external evidence. In my view, the internal evidence should certainly take precedence in the case of the Gospel of John, not least because the external evidence is hardly unequivocal. This does not alleviate the necessity of explaining how the Gospel came to be ascribed to someone named John, but we will leave that question to the end of our discussion.

As far as the external evidence goes, it is true enough that there were various church fathers in the second century who thought John son of Zebedee was the author. There was an increasing urgency about this conclusion for the mainstream church after the middle of the second century, because the Fourth Gospel seems to have been a favorite amongst the Gnostics, and therefore, apostolic authorship was deemed important if this gospel was to be rescued from the heterodox. Irenaeus, the great heresiarch, in particular around A.D. 180 stressed that this gospel was written in Ephesus by one of the Twelve—John. It is therefore telling that this seems not to have been the conclusion of perhaps our very earliest witness—Papias of Hierapolis, who was surely in a location and in a position to know something about Christianity in the provenance of Asia at the beginning of the second century A.D. Papias ascribes this gospel to one elder John, whom he distinguishes presumably from another John, and it is only the former that he claims to have had personal contact with. Eusebius, in referring to the Preface to Papias's five-volume work, stresses that Papias only had contact with an elder John and one Aristion, not with John of Zebedee (*Hist. Eccl.* 3.39-3-7), who is distinguished by Eusebius himself from the John in question. It is notable as well that Eusebius reminds us that Papias reflects the same chiliastic eschatology as is found in the book of Revelation, something that Eusebius looks askance at. Eusebius is clear that Papias only knew the "elders" who had had contact with the "holy apostles," not the "holy apostles" themselves. Papias had heard personally what Aristion and the elder John were saying, but had only heard about what the earlier apostles had said.

As most scholars have now concluded, Papias was an adult during the reign of Trajan and perhaps also Hadrian, and his work that Eusebius cites should probably be dated to about A.D. 100 (see the *ABD* article on Papias), which is to say only shortly after the Fourth Gospel is traditionally dated. All of this is interesting in several respects. In the first place, Papias does not attempt to claim too much, even though he has great interest in what all the apostles and the Twelve have said. His claim is a limited one of having heard those who had been in contact with such eyewitnesses. In the second place, he is writing at a time and in a place where he ought to have known who it was that was responsible for putting together the Fourth Gospel, and equally clearly he reflects the influence of the millennial theology we find only clearly in the book of Revelation in the New Testament and not, for example, in the Fourth Gospel. This suggests that the John he knew and had talked with was John of Patmos, and this was the same John who had something to do with the production of the Fourth Gospel. It is significant that Hengel, after a detailed discussion in his *The Johannine Question*, concludes that this gospel must be associated with the elder John who was not the same as John son of Zebedee. More on this in due course. As I have stressed, while Papias's testimony is significant and early, we must also give due weight to the internal evidence in the Fourth Gospel itself, to which we will turn shortly. One more thing. Papias Fragment 10.17 has now been subjected to detailed analysis by M. Oberweis,[5] and Oberweis, rightly in my judgment, draws the conclusion that Papias claimed that John son of Zebedee died early as a martyr like his brother (Acts 12:2). This counts against both the theory that John of Patmos was John of Zebedee and the theory that the latter wrote the Fourth Gospel. But I defer to my friend and colleague Richard Bauckham whose new book is a wealth of information about Papias, and his conclusion is right—we should take very seriously what Papias says. He knew what he was talking about in regard to both the earliest and latest of the gospels.[6]

Andrew Lincoln, in his new commentary on the Gospel of John, has concluded that the Beloved Disciple was a real person and "a minor follower of Jesus during his Jerusalem ministry."[7] While Lincoln sees the Beloved Disciple traditions as added to the Gospel as small snippets of historical tradition added to a larger core that did not come from this person, he draws this conclusion about the Beloved Disciple's provenance for a very good reason—he does not show up at all in this Gospel in the telling of the Galilean ministry stories, and on the other hand he seems to be involved with and know personally about Jesus' ministry in and around Jerusalem.

One of the things that is probably fatal to the theory that John son of Zebedee is the Beloved Disciple and also the author of this entire document is that none, and I do mean none, of the special Zebedee stories are included in the Fourth Gospel (e.g. the calling of the Zebe-dees by Jesus, their presence with Jesus in the house where Jesus raised Jairus's daughter, the story of the transfiguration, and also of the spe-cial request for special seats in Jesus' kingdom when it comes, and we could go on). In view of the fact that this gospel places some stress on the role of eyewitness testimony (see especially John 19-21), it is passing strange that these stories would be omitted if this Gospel were by John of Zebedee, or even if he was its primary source. It is equally strange that the Zebedees are so briefly mentioned in this gospel as such (see John 21:2), and John is never equated with the Beloved Dis-ciple even in the appendix in John 21 (cf. verses 2 and 7—the Beloved Disciple could certainly be one of the two unnamed disciples men-tioned in verse 2).

Also telling is the fact that this gospel includes none or almost none of the special Galilean miracle stories found in the Synoptics with the exception of the feeding of the 5,000/walking on water tandem. The author of this document rather includes stories like the meeting with Nicodemus, the encounter with the Samaritan woman, the healing of the blind man, the healing of the cripple by the pool, and the raising of Lazarus, and what all these events have in common is that *none of them transpired in Galilee*. When we couple this with the fact that our author seems to have some detailed knowledge about the topography in and around Jerusalem and the historical particulars about the last week or so of Jesus' life (e.g. compare the story of the anointing of Jesus by Mary of Bethany in John to the more generic Markan account), it is not a surprise that Lincoln and others reflect a growing trend recognizing the Judean provenance of this gospel. Recognition of this provenance clears up various difficulties not the least of which is the lack of Galilean stories in general in this gospel and more particularly the lack of exorcism tales, none of which, according to the Synoptics, are said to have occurred in Jerusalem or Judea. Furthermore, there is absolutely no emphasis or real interest in this gospel in the Twelve as Twelve or as Galileans. If the author is a Judean follower of Jesus and is not one of the Twelve, and in turn is sticking to the things he knows personally or has heard directly from eyewitnesses, this is understandable. This brings us to the question of who this Beloved Disciple might have been.

It has been common in Johannine commentaries to suggest that the Beloved Disciple as a figure in the narrative does not show up under that title before John 13. While this case has been argued thoroughly, it overlooks something very important. This gospel was written in an oral culture for use with non-Christians as a sort of teaching tool to lead them to faith. It was not intended to be handed out as a tract to the nonbeliever, but nevertheless its stories were meant to be used orally for evangelism. In an oral document of this sort, the ordering of things is especially important. Figures once introduced into the narrative by name and title or name and identifying phrase may thereafter be only identified by one or the other since economy of words is at a premium when one is writing a document of this size on a piece of papyrus (John 20:30-31). This brings us to John 11:3 and the phrase *hon phileis*. It is perfectly clear from a comparison of 11:1 and 3 that the sick person in question first called Lazarus of Bethany and then called "the one whom you love" is the same person, as, in the context, the mention of sickness in each verse makes this identification certain. This is the first time in this entire gospel that any particular person is said to have been loved by Jesus. Indeed one could argue that this is the only named person in the whole Gospel about whom this is specifically said directly. This brings us to John 13:23.

At John 13:23 we have the by now very familiar reference to a disciple whom Jesus loved (*hon agapa* this time) as reclining on the bosom of Jesus, by which is meant he is reclining on the same couch as Jesus. The disciple is not named here, and notice that nowhere in John 13 is it said that this meal transpired in Jerusalem. It could just as well have transpired in the nearby town of Bethany, and this need not even be an account of the Passover meal. John 13:1, in fact, says it was a meal that transpired *before* the Passover meal. This brings us to a crucial juncture in this discussion. In John 11 there is a reference to a beloved disciple named Lazarus. In John 12 there was a mention of a meal at the house of Lazarus. If someone were hearing these tales in this order without access to the Synoptic Gospels, it would be natural to conclude that the person reclining with Jesus in John 13 is Lazarus. There is another good reason to conclude so. It was the custom in this sort of dining that the host would recline with or next to the chief guest. The story as we have it told in John 13 likely implies that the Beloved Disciple is the host. But this in turn means he must have a house in the vicinity of Jerusalem. This in turn probably eliminates *all* the Galilean disciples.

This identification of the Beloved Disciple as Lazarus in fact not only clears up some conundrums about this story, it also neatly clears up a series of other conundrums in the Johannine Passion Narrative as well. For example: (1) it was always problematic that the Beloved Disciple had ready access to the high priest's house. Who could he have been to have such access? Surely not a Galilean fisherman. John 11:36-47 suggests that some of the Jewish officials who reported to the high priest had known Lazarus and had attended his mourning period in Bethany. This in turn means that Lazarus likely had some relationship with them. He could have had access to Caiphas's house, being a high-status person known to Caiphas's entourage; (2) if Lazarus of Bethany is the Beloved Disciple, this too explains the omission of the Garden of Gethsemane prayer story in this Gospel. Peter, James, and John were present on that occasion, but the Beloved Disciple was not; (3) it also explains John 19:27. If the Beloved Disciple took Jesus' mother "unto his own" home (it is implied), this surely suggests some locale much nearer than Galilee, for the Beloved Disciple will show up in Jerusalem in John 20 immediately thereafter, and of course Mary is still there, according to Acts 1:14, well after the crucifixion and resurrection of her son; (4) how is it that the Beloved Disciple gets to the tomb of Jesus in John 20 before Peter? Perhaps because he knows the locale, indeed knows Joseph of Arimathea and Nicodemus, being one who lived near and spent much time in Jerusalem. One more thing about John 20:2, which Tom Thatcher kindly reminded me of. Here the designation of our man is a double one—he is called both "the other disciple" and also the one "whom Jesus loved," only this time it is *phileō* for the verb. Why has our author varied the title at this juncture, if in fact it was a preexisting title for someone outside the narrative? We would have expected it to be in a fixed form if this were some kind of preexisting title. Notice now the chain of things—Lazarus is identified in John 11 as the one whom Jesus loves, and here "the other disciple" (see John 20:1-2) is identified as the one whom Jesus loves, which then allows him to be called "the other disciple" in the rest of this segment of the story. But at 20:2 we return once more to his main designation—the one whom Jesus loved (=Lazarus). All of this makes good sense if John 11–21 is read or heard in the sequence we now find it; (5) of course the old problem of the fact that the Synoptics say all the Twelve deserted Jesus once he was taken away for execution, even Peter, and record only women being at the cross, is not contradicted by the account in John 19 if in fact the Beloved Disciple, while clearly enough from John 19:26 a man (called Mary's "son," and so not Mary Magdalene!), is Lazarus rather than one of the Twelve; (6) there is the further point that if indeed the Beloved Disciple took Mary into his own home, then we know where the Beloved Disciple got the story of the wedding feast at Cana—he got it from Mary herself. I could continue mounting up small particulars of the text that are best explained by the theory of Lazarus's being the Beloved Disciple, but this must suffice. I want to deal with some larger issues in regard to this Gospel that are explained by this theory, in particular its appendix in John 21 But one more conjecture is in order here.

Scholars of course have often noted how the account of the anointing of Jesus in Bethany as recorded in Mark 14:3-11 differs from the account in John 12:1-11, while still likely being the same story or tradition. Perhaps the most salient difference is that Mark tells us that the event happens in the home of Simon the Leper in Bethany, while John 12 indicates it happens in the house of Mary, Martha, and Lazarus in Bethany. Suppose for a moment, however, that Simon the Leper was in fact the father of these three siblings. Suppose that Lazarus himself, like his father, had also contracted the dread disease and succumbed to it (and by the way we now know for sure that the deadly form of

Hansen's disease did exist in the first century A.D.). Now this might well explain why it is that none of these three siblings seems to be married. Few have commented on why this trio of adults did not have families of their own, but are rather still living together; but it is not at all odd if the family was plagued by a dread disease that made them unclean on an ongoing or regular basis. It also explains why these folks never travel with Jesus' other disciples, who never get near this family until that fateful day recorded in John 11 when Jesus raised and healed Lazarus. Jesus of course was not put off by the disease and so had visited the home previously alone (Luke 10:38-42). But other early Jews would certainly not have engaged in betrothal contracts with this family if it was known to be a carrier of leprosy.

Most scholars are in agreement that John 21 makes clear that while the Beloved Disciple is said to have written down some gospel traditions, he is no longer alive when at least the end of this chapter was written. The "we know his testimony is true" is a dead giveaway that someone or someones other than the Beloved Disciple put this Gospel into its final form and added this appendix, or at a minimum added the story about the demise of the Beloved Disciple and the conclusion of the appendix. This line of reasoning I find compelling. And it also explains something else. We may envision that whoever put the memoirs of the Beloved Disciple together is probably the one who insisted on calling him that. In other words, the Beloved Disciple is called such by his community perhaps and by his final editor certainly, and this is not a self-designation, indeed was unlikely to be a self-designation in a religious subculture where humility and following the self-sacrificial, self-effacing example of Jesus were being inculcated. This then explains one of the salient differences between 2 and 3 John and the Gospel of John. The author of those little letters calls himself either the "elder" or "the old man" depending on how you want to render *presbyteros*. He nowhere calls himself the Beloved Disciple, not even in the sermon we call 1 John, where he claims to have personally seen and touched the Word of Life, which in my view means he saw and touched Jesus. We must reckon then with at least two persons being responsible for the final form of the Fourth Gospel while only one is necessary to explain the *epiphenomena* of the Johannine Epistles. This brings us to the story itself in John 21:20-24.

Why is the final editor of this material in such angst about denying that Jesus predicted that the Beloved Disciple would live until Jesus returned? Is it because there had been a tradition in the Beloved Disciple's church that he would, and if so, what generated such a tradition? Not apparently the Beloved Disciple himself. But now he has passed away, and this has caused anxiety among the faithful about what was the case with the Beloved Disciple and what Jesus had actually said about his future in A.D. 30. I would suggest that no solution better explains all the interesting factors in play here than the suggestion that the Beloved Disciple was someone that Jesus had raised from the dead, and so quite naturally there arose a belief that surely he would not die again before Jesus returned. Such a line of thought makes perfectly good sense if the Beloved Disciple had already died once and the second coming was still something eagerly anticipated when he died. Thus I submit that the theory that Lazarus was the Beloved Disciple and the author of most of the traditions in this Gospel is a theory that best clears up the conundrum of the end of the appendix written after his death.

And finally there is one more thing to say. It is of course true that the Fourth Gospel takes its own approach to presenting Jesus and the gospel tradition. I am still unconvinced by the attempts of Lincoln and others to suggest that the author drew on earlier gospels, particularly Mark. I think he may have known of such gospels, may even have read Mark, but is certainly not dependent on the Synoptic material for his own gospel. Rather he takes his own line of approach and has an abundance of information that he is unable to include in his gospel, including much non-Synoptic material (see John 20:30 and 21:25) because of the constraints of writing all this down on one papyrus. He did not need to boil up his gospel based on fragments and snippets from the Synoptics. On the contrary, he had to be constantly condensing his material, as is so often the case with an eyewitness account that is rich in detail and substance. But it is not enough to say that the author was an eyewitness to explain this gospel's independence and differences from the earlier Synoptic Gospels. There are other factors as well.

As I pointed out over a decade ago, this gospel is written in a way that reflects an attempt to present the Jesus tradition in the light of the Jewish sapiential material.[8] Jesus is presented as God's wisdom come in the flesh in this gospel, serving up discourses like those of wisdom in earlier Jewish Wisdom literature, rather than offering aphorisms and parables as in the Synoptics. I have suggested that this reflected Jesus' in-house modus operandi for his private teaching with his own inner circle of disciples. We need not choose between the public form of wisdom discourse found in the Synoptics (i.e., parables and aphorisms) and the private form of discourse (see e.g., John 14–17) in John when trying to decide which went back to the historical Jesus—both did, but they had different *Sitz im Lebens* and different functions. But I have concluded that even this line of thinking is insufficient to explain the differences from the Synoptics we find in the Fourth Gospel. There is one more factor in play.

Our author, the Beloved Disciple, had been raised not merely from death's door, but from being truly dead—by Jesus! This was bound to change his worldview, and did so. It became quite impossible for our author to draw up a veiled messiah portrait of Jesus like we find in Mark. No, our author wanted and needed to shout from the mountain tops that Jesus was the resurrection, not merely that he performed resurrections, but that he was what E. Käsemann once said about the presentation of Jesus in the Fourth Gospel—he was a God bestriding the stage of history. Just so, and our author pulls no punches in making that clear in various ways in this Gospel, especially by demonstrating that everything previously said to come only from God, or from the mind and plan of God known as God's wisdom, is now said of and said to come from Jesus. He is the incarnation of the great I AM.

The Beloved Disciple would not have been best pleased with modern minimialist portraits of the historical Jesus. He had had a personal and profound encounter of the first order with both the historical

Jesus and the risen Jesus and knew that they were one and the same. This was bound to change his worldview. It is no accident that the book of Signs in the Fourth Gospel (i.e., John 2–11) climaxes with the story of Lazarus's own transformation, just as the book of glory (John 12–20) climaxes with the transformation of Jesus himself. Lazarus had become what he admired, had been made, to a lesser degree, like Jesus. And he would have nothing to do with mincing words about his risen Savior and Lord. Rather he would walk through the door of bold proclamation, even to the point perhaps of adding the Logos hymn at the beginning of this gospel. This was the Jesus he had known and touched and supped with before and after Easter, and he could proclaim no lesser Jesus.

This leads us to the last bit of the puzzle that can now be solved. How did this gospel come to be named according to John? My answer is a simple one—it is because John of Patmos was the final editor of this gospel after the death of Lazarus. Once Domitian died, John returned to Ephesus and lived out his days. One of the things he did was edit and promulgate the Fourth Gospel on behalf of the Beloved Disciple. Somewhere very near the end of John's own life, Papias had contact with this elderly John. It is not surprising, since this contact seems to be brief, that Papias learned correctly that this John was not the Zebedee John and that this elderly John had something to do with the production of the Fourth Gospel. This I think neatly explains all of the various factors involved in our conundrum. It may even have been Papias who was responsible for the wider circulation of this gospel with a tag "according to John." It is not surprising that Irenaeus, swatting buzzing Gnostics like flies, would later conclude that the Fourth Gospel must be by an apostle or one of the Twelve.

If I am right about all this, it means that the historical figure of Lazarus is more important than we have previously imagined, both due to his role in founding churches in and around Ephesus and of course his role in the life of Jesus and Jesus' mother. Jesus must have trusted him implicitly to hand over his mother to him when he died. Lazarus was far more than one additional recipient of a miraculous healing by Jesus. He was "the one whom Jesus loved" as the very first reference to him in John 11 says. We have yet to take the measure of the man.

What then are the ramifications of this for our study of John 13–17? For one thing, we now have a clear answer to suggest as to why we don't have a detailed depiction of the Passover meal as modified by Jesus on Maundy Thursday night. Our author, the Beloved Disciple, was present earlier in the week at the meals that took place in his house (see John 12), and we can now suggest that the meal referred to in John 13 is also in the house in Bethany. It is not the same meal as the one at which Jesus was betrayed. This explains why we have the footwashing story in John 13 but no reference to the Passover elements and Jesus' modifications on the one hand, and why the latter is precisely what we have in the Synoptics with no reference whatsoever to footwashing. Two different meals were being described, and the Beloved Disciple, while possibly present at all these meals, including the one in Jerusalem in the upper room (see 13:23), focuses on the earlier meal. His purpose is entirely different in John 13–17 than we find in the Synoptics. He wants us to know about other things Jesus said and did during the last week of his life, things that reveal what sort of person and sage Jesus really was. Thus at 13:18 he segues to the second important meal of that week, the Last Supper, without reference to the Passover elements themselves. As we bear these things in mind, a few other things begin to come together.

CRY OF THE BELOVED–JOHN 13 IN A NEW LIGHT

Let us consider more closely the parallels between John 12:1-8 and 13:1-30. In the former story Jesus is anointed on the feet, and that action is interpreted as a symbol of his coming death, indeed as a proleptic burial ritual. In John 13 Jesus himself washes the feet of his disciples, and this is seen as a foreshadowing of both the coming death of Jesus, by which all who believe in him will be made clean, and in particular the cleansing of Peter, which foreshadows his future need for cleansing and restoration after his denials of Christ. Peter is depicted as fallible but redeemable, whilst Judas is portrayed by contrast as one who becomes possessed by Satan and chooses darkness over light. When he goes forth to do his dastardly deed, it is suddenly said to be "night" (13:30). John 13:1-30 must be seen as having extensive links with what comes before and after it, with the Beloved Disciple and actions involving feet being involved in both John 12 and 13. The two actions are distinguishable of course and serve differing functions, but they share in common a foreshadowing of Jesus' coming death.

Our author is not interested in speaking about the original disciples' participation in a Passover meal with Jesus. Indeed he speaks mainly about a meal that took place earlier in the week, which he himself was the host of and had personal knowledge of. If this is correct, then we should not be debating why the Beloved Disciple's depiction of this meal is so different from the depiction of the Last Supper in the Synoptics and in Paul. They are two different meals. Our author is rather seeking to portray Jesus as a winsome sage who offers still relevant after-dinner discourse to his disciples in the context of a Greco-Roman style meal.

John 13:1 does more than just mention a time reference of an event that occurred "before the festival of the Passover," a phrase that could even mean on the day of Unleavened Bread before the whole weekly Passover festival began, not merely before the day Passover was in fact eaten. Our author stresses that Jesus knew his time was up and his hour to culminate his ministry was at hand. This prepares us for the farewell discourses that follow. It was believed in antiquity that what one said at the end of one's life, or as it was coming to a close, was especially significant, in fact was often viewed as "famous last words." Our author has adeptly set up the discourses so they would be seen in that light.

It is important to our author that he portray Jesus' being in control every step of the way, even to the point of ordering Judas to get on with his treachery (13:27b), a feature not found in the Synoptic accounts of the Last Supper (not least because it was not a part of that meal). John 13:1 is, in fact, a long unwieldy sentence in the Greek. It climaxes with the statement that Jesus loved his disciples *eis telos*, which likely means to the end of his life. This will be demonstrated in the account that follows. This love is shown in the footwashing, in the teaching, in testamentary dispensations for the Beloved Disciple and his mother from the cross. By contrast with this love is the hate that has been put in the heart of Judas, which leads to the betrayal (13:2). The shocking character of this meal lies not just in the announcement that one of the inner circle would betray Jesus, but that the decision to betray took place at the fellowship meal and would involve one sitting very near to Jesus in a place of honor. Irony is placed on top of irony when we are told that the very person who is given the choice morsel, at that moment, decides to betray Jesus. Thus Judas's act violates a basic rule about ancient hospitality that one does not betray or break fellowship with one's host while dining with him, regardless of the animus one bears for the host or special guest (Ps 23:5). Jesus gives Judas a sign of friendship, and Judas chooses that minute to betray him. Our author has brought forward this portion of the Last Supper story into his singular story of a meal followed by discourses. We are apparently meant to think that Jesus even washed Judas's feet, and then Judas still betrayed him.

The justification for this blending of two meal stories and several different discourses is not hard to uncover. In John 13:10-11 Jesus had spoken about not all disciples being clean, and our Evangelist refers this to the one who would betray Jesus. This in turn gives him the segue so that he, in 13:18-38, could portray his interpretation of the betrayal event which actually took place during the Last Supper. John 13:1-17 speaks of something that happened at one meal; 13:18-38 perhaps of the meal later in the week.[9] He wishes to contrast Jesus who is the light, the glorious Wisdom and truth of God, with the darkness that we see in Judas and his false actions.

John 13:3 tells us that Jesus chose to perform the dramatic sign-act of footwashing knowing that he had come from and would go back to the Father, and that furthermore the Father had delivered his fate over into his own hands. Up to this juncture in the story, Jesus has had to wait for the Father's directions or go-ahead before he does something (see John 11:1-2), but now Jesus has control in his own hands. It is thus all the more telling that Jesus wanted to punctuate his modeling of servant leadership right to the end of his ministry. Footwashing was a task reserved for servants, and notice how Jesus even strips down to the Spartan attire of a slave to perform this act, disrobing and tying a towel around his waist. Jesus washes the disciples' feet with water from a basin and then wipes them with a towel.

John 13:6-8 suggests that Peter questioned and then rejected such a lowly action from his Master. This was a role reversal he was not prepared for. It might be appropriate for a pupil to do this for his master, but not the converse. John 13:7 indicates that only later will Peter understand the real significance of this act that points us forward to Peter's denials in John 18 and the story of his restoration in John 21. Jesus tells Peter that unless he washes Peter "you have no share in me" (13:8). The language is that of having a kind of inheritance, and it is further developed at 14:3 and 17:24. Jesus himself is seen as the disciples' promised land, their prized possession. In typical impulsive fashion Peter replies in 13:9 that Jesus should wash his hands and head as well.

John 13:10 has sometimes been thought to refer to both baptism and the later Christian ceremony of footwashing, but as Don Carson says, the focus here is christological, not sacramental.[10] Notice that in 13:11-12 the author clarifies who it is who would betray Jesus, a detail one would presume the Johannine community would not need, but this material was intended for evangelistic purposes. Having performed this symbolic act, Jesus dons his robe and returns to the table. How should we evaluate this act and determine whether it should be part of later Christian practices?

In the first place we must make clear that it has no bearing on the Christian practice of baptism, and if we are right that this was an event that did not take place at the Last Supper, then it is understandable why Paul knows nothing about carrying it forward into the practice of the Lord's Supper in 1 Corinthians 11, nor does Luke in Acts 2. If the ceremony had been meant to symbolize baptism, the feet would not be the obvious prime choice for attention and cleansing.[11] More to the point, we would not expect Jesus to object to pouring water on head and hands if this is a symbol of baptism. Jesus was not an anti-immersionist so far as we know! Rather, the footwashing ceremony points forward to the cleansing that happens through Jesus' death on the cross. Jesus is making graphic through this symbolic act the lengths he will go as a servant to cleanse his disciples from sin.

If we are to reflect on the relationship between footwashing and the later Last Supper meal, then one would say that footwashing symbolizes the cleansing that is necessary before one partakes of Christ, whereas the bread and the cup symbolize the actual partaking of Christ. In order words, footwashing, which often preceded a meal when a guest came into the house, can symbolize the cleansing necessary before partaking of the Lord's Supper, but it is not part of that meal itself or its symbols. Washing someone's feet can hardly be parallel in significance to the words of institution and the partaking of the Lord's Supper, and it is telling that this ceremony is nowhere else referred to in the New Testament outside of John 13. In view of his lack of interest in sacraments in general (including baptism and the Lord's Supper as Christian practices), we may doubt that our author intends to suggest that Jesus is instituting a new ceremony that his disciples must use. Notice, however, that Jesus does suggest the disciples should wash one another's feet. Does this refer to this ritual or does it refer to the need to offer forgiveness and so the cleansing of sins between believers? It may well just be the latter. Here as elsewhere in this gospel one is encouraged to read the story at a level beyond the material one and look for the large spiritual significance of the story. Jesus asks, "Do you know what I have done to you?" not "Do you understand how to perform this ceremony now?"

The disciples, like Jesus, are to go out into the dark world as servants offering cleansing from sin through Christ. They are blessed if they do the same sort of loving and forgiving and self-sacrificial acts as Jesus does. In short, while the ceremony is not mandated here, nevertheless there is nothing to rule out its being a viable expression of the message of Christ about cleansing and forgiveness.

One final point is worth mentioning. In John 13:23 we see the Beloved Disciple reclining on the bosom of Jesus. This echoes John 1:18, which refers to Jesus being in the bosom of the Father. The suggestion is that the Beloved Disciple stands in an analogous relationship to Jesus as Jesus has with the Father. In other words, this gospel is the personal and eyewitness testimony of one who was close to the heart of Jesus.[12] Thus while this story does not really tell us much pertinent to our discussion of the Lord's Supper ceremony itself, it speaks volumes about Jesus himself who took the form of a servant and was obedient even unto death on the cross for the cleansing of our sins.

Rites like baptism and ceremonies like the Lord's Supper and even footwashing are in a sense the Word made visible. And in an age of visual learners, they become more important, not less, to our understanding not merely of the sacraments but of the whole import and nature of Christ and his story. This was brought home vividly to me when I was asked on one occasion to preach in a Church of the Brethren worship service. I shall not soon forget the occasion. The service went well enough, and then I was told we were all processing downstairs to the fellowship hall for a meal. This was fair enough, and I was seated at a table with an elderly gentleman, one of the saints of the church. Food was placed on the table but so were the elements of the Lord's Supper, and then the next thing I knew, the elderly gentleman was on his knees beside me, taking off my shoes and socks and beginning to wash my feet before the meal! Being a Methodist, I had never had this experience before. I wanted to protest in the same way Peter had done—"no sir, I should be doing this for you." It seemed all wrong on first blush. And then I remembered John 13 and realized that the story had taken on flesh right before my eyes. I had become part of that story. I was instantly humbled and honored to be served by that elderly man, and realized it was just what Jesus would have done as well. Indeed, he was doing it through his agent and disciple on that day.

I was reminded in a telling way that ceremonies, if one partakes of them in an open and worthy manner, are more than just sign language, more than just symbols. They are opportunities for a spiritual interchange that produces communion with Christ and with one another. Perhaps we need more ceremonies, not fewer, more occasions to enact and depict our faith and serve one another. For if the Lord of Hosts is the Host and unseen guest at his own Table, then we too have a rebirth of understanding and wonder when it comes to such ceremonies. This is not because there is something magical about the ceremony, or because it has some inherent dose of grace to pass along. It is because Jesus meets us on such occasions, and there cannot but be blessing and communion and cleansing that happens. And that is something we all need with regularity. We will say more about this in the following chapters.

Chapter 5

MISSING SUPPER

The Eucharist in Early Christianity

Let poor persons and strangers be acquainted with your modest table, and with them Christ shall be your guest.

—Jerome (*Letter 52* to Nepotian)

It is a frustrating fact that we have almost no evidence about how the church viewed the Lord's Supper in the last third of the first century A.D. There are, of course, certain things we can conclude by close analysis of the gospel accounts of the Last Supper, which in small measure reflect the later Christian theology about the Lord's Supper, perhaps especially in Luke's account. Indeed it is a precarious business to assume too much on this front, for the Lord's Supper was not a Passover meal, and it did not simply repeat the protocol of the Jewish meal, nor repristinate all its symbolic elements, as we have seen in this study already.

SLIM PICKINGS

If we turn to the rest of the New Testament, we find very little trace, if any, of a discussion about the Lord's Supper. Thank goodness for the problems in Corinth, or we might not have any extended discussions outside the Gospels! Let us review the few texts sometimes thought to allude to the Lord's Supper in the rest of the New Testament.

Firstly there is Jude 12 where we have the reference to the love feasts. *Agapē* feasts were apparently at this time the larger meal context for the celebration of the Lord's Supper and seem to have involved a fellowship meal (cf. 1 Cor 11:20-34; Acts 2:46). Apparently, these were evening meals (Acts 20:7, 11) and involved various sorts of intimate sharing with one another.[1] Here the meal is only mentioned because false teachers have infiltrated. Obviously having a "betrayer" in the midst of this sort of setting where everyone is open and trusting was especially dangerous to the church, just as we have seen depicted in the story of the Last Supper in the Gospels. Because these false teachers are men without scruples (*aphobōs*—literally "without fear," possibly meaning without reverence, though it may mean that they would not have scruples against taking advantage of Christians in such a situation), they are especially dangerous. The word *poimaiountes* refers to the fact that these people are supposed to be shepherds looking after others, but in fact they are only looking after (shepherding) themselves, feeding themselves. They are egocentric to the core. There is perhaps an echo here of Ezekiel 34:2-4, 9 (cf. Isa 56:11), which speaks of the shepherds who feed themselves instead of their flocks. But alas, while we learn that these sort of in-house Christian meals were continuing when and where Jude wrote (which I take to be in the 50s in the Holy Land, perhaps Galilee) we really learn nothing additional or new about the Lord's Supper from this text; indeed it is not absolutely certain it is alluded to at all here.

The phrase *love feast*, however, does suggest a distinctively Christian meal characterized by the sort of love and fellowship that should be exhibited in Christian communities. The meal is seen as the especial opportunity to exhibit the values and virtues of the Christian life, indeed exhibit loving the brothers and sisters by means of free and open hospitality. The problem was that when the meal was that open and loving, one's guard would be down, especially since the meal was supposed to be open even to those on the fringes of the community, including perhaps the poor and the slaves. In such a socially porous environment it would not be hard for false teachers claiming to be Christians to slip in and freeload, and cause trouble. Whatever else one can say, these meals were not closely policed. There were no bouncers with guest lists. In this regard they were nothing like some of the closed and by-invitation-only meals of associations, secret societies, or the mystery religions. Christianity was an evangelistic religion, and so this meant risk for the Christian community because they were open to having guests and strangers attend their meetings.

It is perhaps worth pointing out that the practice of offering hospitality including meals, which begins with Jesus and his disciples and continues throughout the New Testament era, was an ongoing feature of the Christian community that really helped the Christian cause of evangelism right up to and beyond the end of the Roman Empire as a pagan entity. For example, Julian the Apostate, the Roman emperor after Constantine, who tried to turn back the clock and reinstitute full-fledged paganism in the Empire, in about A.D. 362, instructed various of the pagan priests to imitate the Christians and their concern for hospitality and the care for the poor and strangers. Calling Christianity "atheism" (by which was meant disbelief in the pagan gods), he asks these priests, "Why do we not observe that it is their benevolence to strangers, their care for the graves of the dead, and the pretended holiness of their lives that have done most to increase atheism? . . . For it is disgraceful that, when no Jew ever has to beg, and the impious Galileans [i.e., Christians] support not only their own poor but ours as well, all men see that our people lack aid from us. Teach those of the Hellenic [i.e., pagan] faith to contribute to public service of this sort."[2]

Some have occasionally found a reference to the Lord's Supper in Hebrews 13:10, which says, "We have an altar from which those who officiate in the tent have no right to eat." Is this a reference to the sacrifice of Christ as pledged to believers in the Lord's Supper? The problems with this conclusion are severalfold. As I. H. Marshall points out, our author is referring to a sin offering on the altar, which cannot be eaten precisely because it is a sin offering. The animals were slain away from the altar and burned. Only their blood was poured out on the altar itself. Furthermore, Christians did not have temples or altars since they met in homes, unless one thinks of a Gentile home with a formerly pagan home altar or shrine. But this does not suit the book of Hebrews, which is addressed to Jewish Christians in Rome in the 60s.[3] It is more likely that our author is thinking of the heavenly altar where Christ now serves and provides believers with spiritual sustenance. Non-Christians have no such access to these blessings. In other words, this text is not about the Lord's Supper at all.[4]

And search as we may in the rest of the book of Acts, Pauline letters other than 1 Corinthians, non-Pauline letters, or the book of Revelation, we really find nothing of consequence about the Lord's Supper, nothing that really adds to what we have been able to deduce from a close reading of the gospels, Acts 2, and 1 Corinthians. But is there extracanonical evidence that may help us? The answer is perhaps, and we turn to it now.

THANKSGIVING MEALS IN THE DIDACHE

Toward the end of the nineteenth century a great stir was caused by the publication of a little document today called the Didache, or the "Teaching of the Twelve Apostles" (alternate title—"The Teaching of the Lord through the Twelve Apostles to the Gentiles").[5] This document was immediately declared to be one of the most important (and early) extracanonical Christian writings, and perhaps most scholars would see it that way today, as it is still dated to the end of the first or beginning of the second century by most scholars. I quite agree with this assessment. The provenance of this document is hard to determine specifically, but since in Didache 9.4 we hear about wheat growing on "hills," many have thought it comes from Syria, which is certainly possible. I would suggest we need to consider Galilee itself, especially in view of the Jewish Christian character of the material.[6] The allusion to bread on the hills also might be reminiscent of the feeding of the five thousand in Galilee.

Our interest in this little church manual centers on Didache 9–10 and a bit of Didache 14. It should be first noted that this is indeed a church manual, and the discussion of baptism in Didache 7,[7] followed by a discussion of fasting in Didache 8, brings us to Didache 9–10 in which a thanksgiving meal called the *eucharistias* (9.1) is discussed. It is clear from the outset that a community and communal meal is in view, not just any sort of meal, or even a private Christian meal. The instructions are about how to give thanks at such a meal. At this juncture we need to quote the text fairly extensively and are following Bart Ehrman's translation with some small modifications:

> You shall give thanks as follows. First with respect to the cup: "We give you thanks, our Father, for the holy vine of David, your child, which you made known to us through Jesus your child. To you be the glory forever." And with regard to the fragment of bread "We give you thanks, our Father, for the life and knowledge that you made known to us through Jesus your child. To you be glory forever. As this fragment was scattered upon the mountains and was gathered to become one, so may your church be gathered together from the ends of the earth into your Kingdom. For the glory and power are yours through Jesus Christ forever." But let no one eat or drink from your thanksgiving meal unless they have been baptized in the name of the Lord. For also the Lord has said "Do not give what is holy to the dogs."

The text continues in Didache 10 as follows:

> And when you have had enough to eat, you should give thanks as follows: "We give thanks, holy Father, for your holy name which you

have made reside in our hearts, and for the knowledge, faith, and immortality/deathlessness that you made known to us through Jesus your child. To you be glory forever. You O Master, Almighty created all things for the sake of your name, and gave both food and drink to humans for their refreshment, that they might give you thanks. And you graciously provided us with spiritual food [*pneumatikēn trophēn*] and drink and eternal life through your child. Above all we thank you because you are powerful. To you be the glory forever. Remember your assembly [*ekklēsias*] O Lord; save it from all evil, and perfect it in your love. And gather it from the four winds into your Kingdom, which you prepared for it. For yours is the power and glory forever. May grace come and this world pass away. Hosanna to the God of David. If anyone is holy let them come; if anyone is not, let him repent *Marantha!* Amen." But permit the prophets to give thanks as often as they wish.

Finally from Didache 14 at the end of the document we have:

On the Lord's own day, when you gather together, break bread and give thanks after you have confessed your unlawful deeds, that your sacrifice may be pure. Let no one quarreling with his neighbor join you until they are reconciled, that your sacrifice may not be defiled. For this is the sacrifice mentioned by the Lord: "In every place and time, bring me a pure sacrifice. For I am a great King, says the Lord, and my name is considered marvelous among the Gentiles."

While there are many imponderables about these passages in the Didache, a few things seem clear. Firstly, the instructions given in Didache 10–11 are almost entirely about prayer. Only at the very end of Didache 10 and 11 and in Didache 14, where we see the influence of Jesus' teaching found in Matthew 5:23-24 coupled with a final quote from Malachi 1:11, 14 do we have some actual instructions that involve something other than prayer. Our author's primary concern is about the sort of prayers that should be offered at the meal.

Secondly, there can be no doubt that we are talking about a meal shared by the community, not just any sort of meal, and in view of what is said in some of the prayer material, it seems very probable that our author envisions the Lord's Supper being a part of this meal. Eternal life and knowledge and other blessings are said to be coming through God's child, Jesus, and the repeated reference to Jesus' being the mediator of these blessings points us in the direction of the Lord's Supper. So, too, does the reference to spiritual food, the praying at length over both wine and bread (an interesting order of things). There may be an allusion to the manna scattered and then gathered, or even the feeding of the five thousand, and an analogy drawn with the bread in the Lord's Supper such as we saw in 1 Corinthians 10.

Notice as well that the meal is seen as a time where the unity of the community of Jesus' followers is both recognized and prayed for. This comports with what we saw was the function of the Lord's Supper in 1 Corinthians 11. Furthermore, here the meal is seen as something exclusive. Only the baptized should be allowed to partake of it. Is this warning because of the problems we see in a text like Jude 12? Is the author trying to tighten up the rules about administration of the meal and its proper recipients? It would seem so. Only the holy should come to the meal; the "dogs" should stay away, and again a Matthean saying of Jesus is quoted (Matt 7:6).

One of the more telling features of this material is its eschatological orientation. Whilst Paul mentions celebrating the meal "until he comes" and we have conjectured that the marantha prayer may well have been part of the celebration of the Lord's Supper in Paul's community, here this is certainly the case. We also have reference to the gathering of the church from the four corners of the earth into God's kingdom twice, with the kingdom viewed as future. The entire ethos of this document is like what we find in Jude and Matthew, and to some extent James. In other words, it comes from Jewish Christian circles probably in the Holy Land. And what this document attests is that Jewish Christianity continued to be developing at the end of the first century. It had its own traditions about how to celebrate the

Lord's Supper, still seen as something done in the context of a meal that provides spiritual benefit, communion, and is meant to unite the community. There is certainly nothing here that suggests some sort of magical view of the elements, and we have no commentary at all about the words of institution that Jesus himself spoke. What we do have is the clear statement that Jesus himself (not the meal) is the one who provides everlasting life and the benefits of salvation. These benefits are given thanks for in the meal, not provided by the meal or its celebration. Notice that the thanksgiving is given for the bread and for the drink and also for the gift of eternal life. The former gifts are not seen as the means of receiving the latter more crucial and permanent gift. All these gifts come from and through Jesus.

In regard to the issue of frequency of celebration and whether there were official celebrants, we have some clues. Didache 14 suggests that on the Lord's Day, presumably on every Lord's Day, such a meal should take place with prayers of thanksgiving. Here for the first time we also have a statement that partaking of the meal should be preceded by the confession of sins. Of course this was implied by the contrast between the holy and the dogs, but in Didache 11 it is made explicit. The ending remark in Didache 11 has sometimes been seen as a later addition, which may be true, but in any case it indicates that prophets should be allowed to speak the official thanksgiving prayer (notice it does not say serve the thanksgiving meal) as often as they wish.

This wonderful little document reassures us that despite the silences of various New Testament documents from the latter part of the first century A.D., the Lord's Supper, in the context of a fellowship, or agape, meal, continued to be important for Christians, and indeed it was as important for Jewish Christians as for Gentiles ones. But this leads to one final remark. We have already mentioned the traditional thanksgiving prayer that accompanied Jewish meals, the so-called Kiddush prayer (thanking God who provides bread from the earth . . .). Some of this prayer material may be a modification and Christianization of such general Jewish prayers. But what is so striking is that nothing here connects the Lord's Supper with the Passover, or explains the relationship of the two meals. Nor is there any real meditation on what Christ said about the bread and the cup. Is this because it was taken for granted that the audience understood such things? It is hard to tell. What we can say is this: if one reads the rest of the Didache, there is some clear polemic against non-Christian Jews and the synagogue. Our author seems to be writing in the same sort of context as Matthew's gospel was written, with the synagogue near at hand. This makes it all the more surprising that nothing is said of the Passover meal, to further distinguish the Christian celebration.

AND SO?

Sometimes silences are pregnant and sometimes not. It is hard to know what to make of the silence of much of the New Testament about the Lord's Supper. Perhaps it is simply an accident of time and circumstance. There was not a felt need to address the matter. What we should not likely conclude is that it was not seen as an important matter in the latter part of the first century A.D. What we can observe is that the Lord's Supper continued to be an in-home ceremony taken in the context of a fellowship meal. We also now know it was important in both Gentile and Jewish contexts in the church in the second half of the first century, and beyond. We see no evidence anywhere in this material that clerics of any kind are in charge of the meal and its distribution. Even in the Didache, prophets, who were mouthpieces for God, are only allowed to say the thanksgiving prayer as often as they like. The low ecclesiology, coupled with the ever-present eschatology, suggest that the Didache does indeed go back to the end of the first century A.D. But one precedent in the Didache does stand out: the Lord's Supper is for baptized Christians, and in particular for those who repent of their sins. We are on the way to the church of the Middle Ages in some respects, but we have not begun to localize or confine grace to the elements of the Lord's Supper itself and then have it controlled by clerics.

Chapter 6

SECOND-CENTURY SACRAMENTS

In the modern church the Lord's Supper is not in the physical sense of the term a meal. It is the hunger of the soul and not the hunger of the body that it is now designed to satisfy. But it began from the Passover, a feast of hungry men, who were to clear the table and to leave nothing; and the Lord's Supper began in the Christian Church as a meal in which physical as well as spiritual hunger was satisfied.

—William Barclay

Hopefully, enough has been said in the first five chapters of this study to make clear that when we are discussing the sources that tell us something about the Lord's Supper, we realize that the later theologies and the later debates (real spiritual presence versus physical presence, transubstantiation versus consubstantiation) are nowhere to be found. The earliest practitioners of the Lord's Supper were Jews, and they were indebted to the way meals were celebrated by their Jewish forebears and their Greco-Roman contemporaries. The church had not yet separated the fellowship meal from the ceremony of the Lord's Supper.

For that matter, worship itself, at least outside of Jerusalem, did not transpire outside of homes where these meals were held and were a part of the worship events, or vice versa.

ISSUES OF POWER AND PURITY

There can be little doubt that the agape, or love, feast was a real meal, hence the warnings about gluttony and drunkenness. Furthermore, it was an evening meal, which in the Greco-Roman world was the main meal of the day, indeed the only main meal of the day. The word *deipnon*, applied to the Lord's Meal, is the word for supper, hence the Lord's Supper. The celebration of the Lord's Supper in homes in the evenings is precisely what we would expect since Christians had to work too: the Lord's Day was not a day off back then, and so worship and fellowship events almost always had to transpire in the evening. We all remember the famous story of poor Eutychus (a slave nickname meaning Lucky) who falls asleep and falls out of the window as Paul's sermon drones on too long in the evening worship service. Listen closely to the account:

> On the first day of the week [literally the "first of the sabbath"] we came together to break bread. Paul spoke to the people and, because he intended to leave the next day, kept on talking until midnight. There were many lamps in the upstairs room where we were meeting. Seated in a window was a young man named Eutychus, who was sinking into a deep sleep as Paul talked on and on. When he was sound asleep, he fell to the ground from the third story and was picked up dead. Paul went down, threw himself on the young man and put his arms around him. "Don't be alarmed," he said. "He's alive!" Then he went upstairs again and broke bread and ate. After talking until daylight, he left. The people took the young man home alive and were greatly comforted. (Acts 20:7-12 NIV)

Here we have clear evidence that the worship transpired in the evening, on the first day of the week (Sunday), and went on for hours.

One of the specific reasons they came together was for the breaking of bread, the meal of the Christian community. It is probable that here we have a reference to the Lord's Supper taken in the context of a meal, just as we did in Acts 2. Breakfast in that world was only a snack, mere bread and a little wine mixed with water. Lunch was taken on the go if one lived in a city. The deipnon was in the evening and was an extended affair, as it still is today in many Mediterranean cultures. Thus "it would be very much more natural for an act of fellowship to begin as a real meal than for it to begin as a ceremony. The word for Supper [applied to the Lord's Meal] is further proof of this."[1]

There is another aspect of first-century Christian practice that needs to be stressed as we move on to discussing second-century views and practice—there is no evidence whatsoever that the Lord's Supper required the presence of apostles or other translocal authority figures. Indeed, as we saw in 1 Corinthians 11, the meal clearly was taking place without Paul, Timothy, or Titus present, and Paul does not in any way condemn this. The problems lay with other aspects of the celebration. We noticed as well in Jude 12 that the author is not present with the audience and has no problems with their celebrating the love feast without him, but he is concerned with the influence and influx of false teachers. The author of the Didache also does not refer to apostolic figures running the thanksgiving meal at the local level, even though the work is titled the "Teaching of the Twelve Apostles."

When exactly did this all change, and what were the social and theological factors that led to the change? The answer seems to be in the second century and: (1) because of the consolidation of ecclesial power in the hands of monarchial bishops and others; (2) in response to the rise of heretical movements such as the Gnostics; (3) in regard to the social context of the Lord's Supper, namely, the agape, or thanksgiving, meal, due to the rise to prominence of asceticism in the church; and (4) because the increasingly Gentile majority in the church was to change how second-century Christian thinkers would reflect on the meal. Thus, issues of power and purity and even ethnicity were to change the views of the Lord's Supper and the way it would be practiced.

A SAMPLING OF THE SMORGASBORD

Though it would be nice to tell you that the second-century church had its sacramental-theological act together and all were "of one accord," this is not actually the case. There were a variety of views expressed about the Lord's Supper ranging from the more symbolic and memorial ideas to the spiritual presence or spiritual-food ideas to the more literalistic language about chewing on the flesh of Jesus and drinking his blood. And sometimes we even find all this language in one writer! This is why I speak of a smorgasbord of ideas being present during this period, of which we can partake only a sampling here.

Let us start with Ignatius of Antioch, clearly a transitional figure in many respects. In about A.D. 110, Ignatius wrote to the church in Smyrna:

> Let that be considered a valid 'thanksgiving' that occurs under the bishop or the one to whom he entrusts it. Let the congregation be wherever the bishop is; just as wherever Jesus Christ is, there also is the 'catholic' [i.e., universal] church. It is not permitted either to baptize or to hold a love feast without the bishop. But whatever he approves is acceptable to God, so that everything you do should be secure and valid. (*Smyr.* 8)

Several observations need to be made about this passage. Notice that Ignatius identifies the thanksgiving meal and the agape meal as one and the same. This is what we thought on the basis of the first-century evidence, but now we have confirmation. Here also for the first time we have a very clear power move. There can be no valid thanksgiving/agape/Lord's Supper unless the bishop or someone he authorizes is there to officiate. We are now well on the way to clericalism and the clerical control of sacraments. Notice the reference to baptism and the love feast together. Both require a bishop or his appointee. The coupling of these two practices here, and only these two, make it virtually certain that, for Ignatius, agape feast=Lord's Supper, or at least the latter is a part of the former.

Sometimes we are helped by the comments of outsiders to see what was going on in Christian worship in the second century. From about the same time frame as Ignatius's comment we have the Roman official Pliny, writing to the Emperor Trajan, who ruled A.D. 98–117, about Christians in Bithynia and what to do with them. He reports,

> They were in the habit of meeting on a certain fixed day before it was light, when they sang in alternate verses a hymn to Christ, as to a god, and bound themselves by a solemn oath not to commit any wicked deeds, but never to commit any fraud, theft, adultery, nor deny a trust when they should be called upon to deliver it up; *after which* it was their custom to separate, and then to reassemble to partake of food, but food of an ordinary and innocent sort. (*Letters* 10.96; my emphasis)

What is intriguing about this is the separation of the meal from the worship event, as well as the worship taking place first thing in the morning on a set day of the week (apparently Sunday). Notice as well the reference to ordinary, harmless food, which suggests the daily staple of bread and wine.

It would be hard for us to overestimate the importance of the adjustments Christians had to make as they sought to have a greater and greater impact on their culture in the second century A.D. Everett Ferguson, an expert in the period, stresses

> [t]he situation required Christians to make many adjustments and reinterpretations in their efforts to communicate with their society. The interpretation of the Lord's Supper was included in these matters influenced by new ways of looking at things. A major aspect was a shift from Jewish thought in terms of function and relationships, to Greek philosophical thought about ontology and substance (where Aristotle had made important analyses)."[2]

But how was a Jewish meal practice grounded in the Passover meal to be translated into Greek philosophical categories, and what were the dangers? Would something get lost in translation, or would something be added in translation? In fact it turned out to involve some of both problems. A cursory glance at Justin Martyr's somewhat confusing reflections will illustrate my point.

Justin (famously martyred in Rome in A.D. 165 and called thereafter Justin Martyr) was born in a Roman colony settlement near Samaria perhaps somewhere near the end of the first century A.D. He had as a major part of his education Hellenistic philosophy, something he tries to put to good use in his debates or dialogues with the Jew Trypho, somewhere in the middle of the second century A.D. Justin understood early Judaism reasonably well, but he sought to convey the gospel to Jews in a basically Jewish way and to others using Greek philosophical categories, and not just the Greek language. For example, he describes the bread of the Lord's Supper as "a memorial (*anamnēsis*) of the incarnation" (*Dial.* 70.4) by which one "remembered his passion" (*Dial.* 117.3). The term *memorial*, which goes back not just to Paul's language about the Lord's Supper but to early Jewish thinking about Passover, does not mean merely bringing something to mind or remembering. It refers in some way to bringing that past story and the divine action of the past into the present such that the present audience becomes part of the story and receives the benefit from such actualization.

When discussing the Lord's Supper ceremony with pagans, however, Justin sings a rather different and more confusing tune in his *First Apology*. The following is a much-debated excerpt from that apology: "We do not receive [the thanksgiving meal] as a common bread and drink. In the same manner as Jesus Christ our Savior became flesh through the Word of God and had flesh and blood for our salvation, so also the food for which thanks was given through his word of prayer, from which our flesh and blood are nourished by metabolism, we have been taught to be the flesh and blood of Jesus" (*Apol.* 1.66.2). On the one hand, this passage suggests that we are still to see the bread and wine as real food that really nourishes us. On the other hand, Justin seems to be saying that we don't view the elements as just common food anymore. Justin connects the prayer over the bread (perhaps he is alluding to Christ's original prayer at the Last Supper) with what it is that makes this the body and blood of Christ. More to the point, his analogy between the incarnation of Christ himself as flesh and blood, which is said to have happened "in the same manner" as the food and wine is flesh and blood, certainly begins to point us forward to the medieval doctrine of the Eucharist. As Ferguson adds, we also see that from the time of Justin on through the Middle Ages the term used to refer to the Lord's Supper was "the thanksgiving" (*eucharistias*), so named, as we saw, because of how Jesus began his act of reinterpreting the Passover. I am in agreement with Ferguson that we should not read too much from the later discussion into Justin's confusing words, as it is not at all clear he is talking about a real and ontological transformation of the elements into the real body and blood of Jesus. But his analogy between the incarnation and the elements in the meal opens the door for such discussion.[3]

Perhaps one of the earliest interpreters of Justin's word was Irenaeus, the great heresiarch. Toward the end of the second century, while swatting down Gnostic arguments like flies, Irenaeus makes some passing comments on the "eucharist" or "thanksgiving meal." We need to bear in mind that he is mostly concerned to affirm the goodness of materiality (i.e., of God's physical creation), as witnessed by the Incarnation, the material nature of the elements in the sacrament, and the resurrection body. In the context of that sort of polemic he says the following:

How can they [i.e., the Gnostics] say that flesh which is nourished from the body of the Lord and from his flesh comes to corruption and does not partake of life? Let them either change their views or avoid offering the bread and wine. But our view is in harmony with the eucharist, and the eucharist confirms our view. We offer to God his own things, proclaiming rightly the communion and unity of flesh and spirit. For as bread from the earth when it receives the invocation of God is no longer common bread but the eucharist, consisting of two things, one earthly and one heavenly, so also our bodies when they partake of the eucharist are no longer corruptible but have the hope of the resurrection to eternity. (*Adv. Her.* 4.18.5)

As Ferguson says, the parallels with Justin in the phrase "no longer common bread" seem clear enough, and like Justin, he sees this bread as still providing physical nourishment. But more clearly than Justin, Irenaeus wishes to stress that the prayer of thanksgiving sanctifies the bread and wine so that while not ceasing to be bread and wine, it also becomes something more—heavenly food. As Ferguson stresses: "Nowhere does Irenaeus make a literal identification of the elements with the body and blood; his point is that Christ, by acknowledging material elements in relation to his body and blood, was affirming that they too were material realities. I would contend that for Irenaeus *there is not a conversion or change in the elements*, but a new reality is added to them by reason of their consecration through calling upon God."[4] This seems a fair reading of the data. We are not yet to the point of what we find in Cyril, bishop of Jerusalem (A.D. 349–378), who says, "the bread and wine of the eucharist before the holy invocation of the worshipful Trinity was simply bread and wine, but when the invocation is done, the bread becomes the body of Christ and the wine the blood of Christ" (*Catech. Mys.* 1.7). Here clearly we have arrived at the idea of the transformation of the elements into something other than what they were before. Cyril draws an analogy with the miracle at Cana when water was turned to wine, and he says that the elements really do become the actual body and blood of Christ, the evidence of the senses to the contrary (*Catech. Mys.* 4.1–6).

Tertullian was certainly one of the most formidable and formative of all the church fathers in the second century, and he would shape the character of various theological discussions, especially among the Latin-speaking Fathers, on a variety of topics for centuries to come. In about A.D. 197 or so he wrote his great *Apologia* in North Africa. What we need to know about Tertullian, who is here defending the love feast, or agape meal, against pagan slanders, is that he was an ascetic—indeed he was to become a Montantist.

> Our dinner shows its idea in its name; it is called by the Greek name for love (*agape*). Whatever the cost, it is gain to spend in piety's name, for with that refreshment we help the needy. . . . Since it turns on the duty of religion, it allows nothing vile, nothing immodest. We do not take our places at the table until we have first tasted prayer to God. Only so much is eaten as satisfies hunger; only so much is drunk as meets the needs of the modest. They satisfy themselves only so far as persons who recall that even during the night they must worship God; they talk as those would who know that the Lord listens. After water for the hands come the lights; and then each, from what he knows of the Holy Scriptures, or from his own heart, is called before the rest to sing to God. (The meaning is to prophesy); so that is the test of how much he has drunk. Prayer in like manner ends the banquet. Then we break up; but not to form groups for violence nor gangs for disorder, nor outbursts of lust; but to pursue the same care for self-control and chastity, as persons who have dined not so much on dinner as on discipline. (*Apol.* 39.16–19)

We should compare the same sort of apologetical remarks in Minucius Felix's writing only a bit later (no later than about A.D. 210), who says, "Our feasts are conducted not only with modesty but in sobriety; for we do not indulge in delicacies, or prolong conviviality with wine [i.e., we do not prolong the convivia, the drinking party] but temper our gaiety with gravity, with chaste conversation" (*Octavius* 31.5).

Several things can be said about these remarks. Notice that once again we have in Tertullian the term *love feast*, and notice as well the emphasis on the feeding of the needy in this meal. It is still a real banquet, a real meal, as well as the context for the Lord's Supper. Notice also the strong emphasis on partaking with moderation. And once again we see that worship takes place at night. In one of the more interesting and novel twists, Tertullian mentions that the participants are asked to come forward and sing to God (the reference to the Scriptures suggests singing a psalm),[5] and this is used as a sort of breathalyzer test! One must suppose that if they started slurring their speech as they cranked up the volume on "Amazing Grace," then everyone knew they had had too much wine! It is clear from this passage and the one from Minucius Felix that one of the criticisms of the church agape was that it was like pagan debauchery at their feasts. We find another remark of a similar sort in the later discussions of Cyprian who refers to "the temperate meal resounding with psalms" (*To Donatus* 16). The more ascetical the church became, the more concern there was about the potential bad witness of the agape, and this in fact was to lead to the separation of the agape from the celebration of the Lord's Supper altogether as it became a "church ceremony" rather than a part of a Christian family meal.

We have reserved to the end here the discussion of the so-called Alexandrian school of Clement and Origen, which begins at the end of the second century and continues on well into the third. It must be stressed from the outset that their entire approach to the Lord's Supper is much of a piece with their approach to Scripture, which is to say they are highly allegorical and figurative when they talk about these things, so it is difficult to know what to make of some of their remarks and how literally to take them. Clement, who lived about A.D. 150–213, like Origen, who also wrote during this period of time, was highly ascetical in his approach to Christianity. Origen, of course, famously castrated himself after thinking this was what Matthew 19:10–12 demanded of him if he wanted to emulate the character of Christ.

Asceticism had many dimensions, and one of them was that it led to the exclusion of women from a lot of church activities, including even the love feast/Lord's Supper celebration in some contexts. It also led to some theologizing about the Lord's Supper that was highly figurative and complex. We will have to consider only a small sample from Clement. It appears that in the Alexandrian church there had developed two different agape meals, one public and one private. The Lord's Supper was still partaken as part of that love feast, but distinctions were being made. The common meal in the home was preceded by acts of worship such as the prayer of thanksgiving. The *pater familias* was seen as the priest of the home. Husband, wife, child, slaves—all partake together of the meal, enjoying with thankful hearts the good gifts of God. But when Clement goes on to speak of the public agape, he says, "To us the word Eucharist has become a term of ritual, whose proper meaning is all but obsolete. To the Greek it was still a word of common life—thanksgiving, the grateful sense of benefits received, of good gifts showered by the good Father on mind and heart and body. 'He that eats and drinks unto the Lord and gives God thanks' [Romans 14:6] . . . so that a religious meal is a Eucharist" (*Paed.* 2.1.10). We have not arrived there yet, but by the middle of the fourth century there would be a debate, and some churches and church councils, such as the Council of Laodicea, would ban the love feast, as the rising tide of asceticism swept over the church and its theology. This was bound to change the whole way the Lord's Supper would be viewed. It became, as Clement says, a religious ceremony confined to a part of the church service in a purpose-built building and controlled by priests. The *coup de grâce* came in A.D. 692 at the Council of Trullian where the agape was banned for life, never to return in the medieval church.

This whole trajectory comports with the increasing emphasis on the elements being something inherently holy or sacred, not ordinary food at all like one would have at home. Consider, for example, the words of Hippolytus in his *Apostolic Tradition* 32.2-3:

And let us all take care that no unbaptized person taste of the Eucharist nor a mouse or other animal, and that none of it at all fall and be lost. For it is the Body of Christ to be eaten by them that believe and not be thought lightly of. For having blessed the cup in the Name of God you did receive it as the anti-type of the Blood of Christ. Wherefore do not spill it, so that no alien spirit lick it up, because you did despise it, and become guilty of the Blood of Christ as one who despises the price with which he has been bought.

God forbid a church should contain an entirely sanctified church mouse who has eaten a bit of the Eucharist! We are not far here from John Chrysostom's remark about burying his teeth in the flesh of Christ and of holding in our hands him who is now seated in heaven with the Father (cf. *Homily of John* 47.1; 46.3; *On the Priesthood* 3.4).

In Clement's fuller discussions of the Lord's Supper, he is prepared to interpret John 6:53-56, a crucial text for the development of later Catholic theology of the Lord's Supper, as follows: the eating of the flesh and the drinking of the blood is a manner of speaking through "symbols" (*symbolon*) and allegories about the partaking of faith and of the promises, and of the Holy Spirit and of the divine Word (*Paed.* 1.6.38, 43-47). He then adds:

> The blood of the Lord is twofold. There is his fleshly blood by which we are ransomed from corruption; and there is the spiritual blood by which we are anointed. And this is to drink the blood of Jesus, to partake of the Lord's immorality. The Spirit is the strength of the Word, as the blood is of the flesh. By analogy, as the wine is mixed with water, so the Spirit is with human beings; the mixed wine and water nourishes unto faith, and the Spirit leads to immortality. And the mixing of both the drink and the Word together is called eucharist, a praiseworthy and beautiful grace. Those partaking of it in faith are sanctified in body and soul. (*Paed.* 2.2.19-20)

We may compare this to Tertullian's remark: "Taking bread and distributing it to his disciples, Jesus made it his own body by saying 'This is my body' that is a 'figure (*figura*) of my body.' On the other hand, there would not have been a figure unless there was a true body" (*Adv. Marc.* 4.40.3-6). Notice how in the same text at 1.14.3 Tertullian says, "The bread . . . represents [his] own proper body." We need to bear in mind that for Clement as for Tertullian the terms *symbol* or *figure* did not have their modern connotations. Neither of these writers is referring to something that is merely a symbol in the modern sense. They are also, however, not saying that those elements are literally the body and blood of Christ though there is some close spiritual connection with Christ's exalted body.

AND SO?

As we have seen, in the second century and going into the third century A.D. there was a smorgasbord of views about the Lord's Supper. There was certainly not a consistent or prevailing witness through these two early centuries that provided a real basis for later Catholic or Orthodox sacramental theology. It does appear, however, that there was a trend toward more literalism about the elements and a trend toward talking about the elements being transformed when one prayed over them.

We still see the Lord's Supper being part of the agape, but the rising tide of asceticism was going to do that in, as was the rising tide of clericalism. Views of the Lord's Supper in the majority Gentile church were bound to change over time, especially with the advent of more and more Christian thinkers trying to use Greek philosophy apologetically to defend and define the gospel. When one gets to Clement or Hippolytus, we are clearly a long way from what we find in Paul and the Gospels, where the influence of the Passover is still strongly present and the meal is seen as a family meal, taken in the home, a memorial meal to remember Jesus' death until his return.

There was *nothing* in the first-century discussion nor much in the second-century discussion that suggests the later debates about transubstantiation and consubstantiation, two different literalist or physicalist interpretations. But by the same token, we have seen evidence throughout that it was believed that some sort of spiritual transaction was involved, some sort of spiritual communion between the believer and other believers, and also between the believer and the Lord. It was not just a matter of symbols in the modern sense of that term. The most essential problem with the developing sacramental theology can be summed up as follows: when the church read texts like John 6 out of their original Jewish and sapiential contexts, it led to absolute distortion of what was meant. Jesus was never talking about chewing his literal flesh or drinking his literal blood. This was simply a later Greek philosophical and even magical approach to these early Jewish texts. Here then is a cautionary reminder—the less Jewish the approach one takes to the Lord's Supper, the more likely one is to be wrong about one's assessment of what is the case about the elements.

We have seen some gatekeeping or fencing-the-table language already beginning to rear its head in this context. One needed to be baptized to take the meal; one needed to repent to take the meal; one needed a bishop or his subordinate to serve the meal. This was to become especially problematic when the church began to suggest that grace was primarily, if not exclusively, available through the hands of the priest and by means of the sacrament. One wonders what Jesus, dining with sinners and tax collectors and then eating his modified Passover meal with disciples whom he knew were going to deny, desert, and betray him, would say about all this. There needs to be a balance between proper teaching so the sacrament is partaken of in a worthy manner and overly zealous policing of the table or clerical control of it.

One may wonder, since nowhere in any of the literature thus far reviewed do we hear about clerics or ministers being called priests, nor of the Lord's Supper being called "the sacrifice of the Mass," where such notions come from. There are various historical factors involved, but here as we draw this chapter to a close, a few can be mentioned.

One of the things that happened when the church moved from meetings in homes to having purpose-built buildings beginning before, but accelerated during, the Constantinian era, is that while the church itself was becoming less Jewish in character, it began to apply a more and more Old Testament hermeneutic to its discussions about church, ministry, and sacraments. The church began to be seen as a temple or basilica, the Lord's Supper began to be seen as a sacrifice, and naturally enough the ones offering the sacrifices, just as in Leviticus, were seen to be priests. There was the further move in this direction when Sunday began to be seen as the Sabbath, another example of this same sort of hermeneutic. There were considerable problems with this whole hermeneutic from the start, since nowhere in the New Testament is there set up a class of priests or clerics to administer any sacraments. Indeed, nowhere was there a clear separation between life in the home and life in church. What has often been missed in the discussions of the effects of all this is that it ruled women out of ministry in the larger church and indeed ruled them out of celebrating the Lord's Supper as well, since in the Old Testament only males were priests and only priests could offer sacrifices.

Too often scholars have thought and even suggested that what happened during and after Constantine was that the church sought to replace the pagan temples, priests, and sacrifices with their own. This is at best a half truth. If this had been primarily what was going on, we would have expected to find priestesses showing up in the mainstream church in and after the time of Constantine, since there were certainly priestesses in the pagan temples. But this we do not find in the historical record. This is because the church of that period was not merely trying to supplant pagan religion with Christian religion, though some of that was going on. More to the point, there was a rising tide of anti-Judaism, and one of its manifestations was this Old Testament hermeneutic. The Torah had been claimed as the church's book, Jews were being ostracized and then later ghettoized, and a hermeneutic of ministry was being adopted which co-opted the Old Testament for church use when it came to priests, temples, and sacrifices, and indeed sacraments in general. Thus ironically enough while the structure of the ecclesial church was becoming more Old Testamental, the church hierarchy was not only becoming less tolerant of Jews, it was forgetting altogether the Jewish character of Jesus' ministry and his modifications of the Passover that led to the Lord's Supper celebration of the early church in the first place.

And one more thing. When the church adopted and adapted an Old Testament vision of ministry, needless to say it became more patriarchal in its vision of ministry in general. Were it not for the monastic movement, the rise of nunneries as well as monasteries, women might have been foreclosed from all forms of ministry in the church during the early medieval period. This also does not comport with what we find in the early-church praxis in Paul's letters and Acts. And it is precisely because of factors such as these—rising clericalism, rising patriarchalism, rising anti-Judaism, the co-opting of Old Testament "ecclesiology"—that modern scholars have spoken about the cultural captivity of the medieval church with some reason. The church had admired and emulated other religious organizations that had done well over the centuries (both pagan and Jewish), and then it became what it admired. In our next chapter we will begin to explore some of the later church's historical Lord's Supper discussions of relevance to this study.

At this point one can say it did not augur well for the celebration of the Lord's Supper when the church went mainstream, ceased to be an illicit religion or countercultural in any real sense, and moved its meal out of the house and into the church and then to the fellowship hall. The church had come a long way since the Last Supper, and much of it had involved a journey away from, and even against, its original Jewish recipe. The result was half-baked sacramental theology with too many foreign flavors overwhelming the main ingredient.

Chapter 7

WHEN THE MEAL BECAME THE MASS

For the early Christians, the reconstituted household provided the setting for the three dimensions of hospitality . . .: hospitality as a means of respect and recognition—in welcoming persons of different status and background into a single place and often a shared meal; hospitality as a means of meeting the physical needs of strangers, traveling Christians, and the local poor; and hospitality as the hosting of local assemblies of believers. These were overlapping and interrelated practices, all located within the household.

—Christine Pohl

What happened when Christianity went public, when worship moved from the house to the basilica, when the Lord's Supper ceased to be set in the context of a meal and seen as part of the Christian agape, and indeed related to Christian hospitality? It cannot be accidental that at the same time the social character of early Christianity was changing in dramatic ways, the theology of the Lord's Supper increasingly changed as well, moving from the concept of a meal to the concept of a sacrifice of the Mass. This even entailed going against the flow of some Old Testament texts, for in the Old Testament at least people brought their own sacrifices to the altar for the priest to deal with. But as things turned out in the church, only priests were to be involved in offering the sacrifice of the Mass. Eventually, of course, these sorts of shifts were also to involve moving from the use of ordinary bread and wine to the use of "communion," or holy, wine and the use of various sorts of bread substitutes, including wafers. Historians of ritual will tell you that when the symbols change, the social reality has changed, or is changing, as well. These things do not happen by accident.

It will be remembered from our discussion of 1 Corinthians 10–11 that Paul used the Lord's Supper and its discussion to work toward the unity of the factious Corinthian congregation. As Wayne Meeks points out, "The single loaf used in the ritual symbolizes the unity of Christ and of the believer with Christ and, consequently, the unity of the community in its participation in Christ (10:17)."[1] "Because . . . we . . . are one body," says Paul, "we all partake of the one loaf." But what happens when there is no longer a single loaf, but rather only individual elements individually received? What happens when the emphasis shifts from the unity of the body and the inclusion of all to the breaking of the elements, and even to the reserving of one of the elements, the wine, for the priest? What happens is the Lord's Supper ceases to have the same function and social significance it had in early Christianity—a true meal shared by Christians and fostering *koinōnia* or communion with one's Lord and one's fellow disciples.

We must take some more time to chronicle a bit the historical journey in the church away from the New Testament significance of the Lord's Meal and discuss what changes happened at the Reformation. As we shall see, while the Reformation brought change, it was not always or necessarily a change that amounted to a return to a more New Testament model of approaching the Lord's Supper.

THE ELEMENTS OF SURPRISE AND GRACE

There was no monolithic teaching or dogma about the Lord's Supper in the early church of the first or second century. And especially in the second century we see a plurality of views and approaches begin to surface. It is worth stressing that there continued to be this variety of views for several centuries thereafter. Two examples will need to suffice. Origen, for example, can take the eating and drinking of the body and blood of Christ to signify the receiving of the teaching and words of Christ, which bring life and nourish the soul (*Hom. On Matt.* 85). Eusebius, the so-called Father of Church History, can write in the fourth century, commenting on John 6.51-52, that in that text flesh and blood refer to the words and sermons of Jesus at that time (*Eccles. Theo.* 3.12). This is actually far more likely to be historically accurate than later highly sacramental readings of those verses.

Yet it was precisely in the fourth century, and not accidentally or incidentally after Constantine became emperor and Christianity came out of the catacombs and into increasing public prominence, that we have Cyril of Jerusalem in the East in about A.D. 347 and Ambrose of Milan in the West in about A.D. 374 both saying that the prayer of consecration turns the ordinary elements into something they were not before. Cyril, speaking to his catechumens, says they must be completely convinced and persuaded that "what seems bread is not bread, though bread by taste, but rather the body of Christ; and that what seems wine is not wine, though the taste will have it so, but rather the blood of Christ." He then goes on to explain how this change is wrought: "We call upon the merciful God to send forth his Holy Spirit upon the gifts lying before him, *that he may make the bread the body of Christ, and the wine the blood of Christ. For whatsoever the Holy Spirit has touched is sanctified and changed*" (*Mystagogical Catecheses* 4.1–9; 5.7 [my emphasis]; the Greek word *metaballesthai* is used in the lattermost verse and means "transformed" or "changed").

We begin to see here wherein the problem lies. The bread and wine continue to appear to be and to taste as if they were bread and wine. So it is assumed there must be some miraculous process, in this case wrought by the Holy Spirit, that transforms the elements into something they were not before. Of course the whole problem with this is that the words Jesus spoke at his modified Passover meal did not in any way suggest a transformation—he simply said "this bread (is) my body" and similarly with the blood. Similarly Ambrose, in seeking to answer the objection "But it still appears to be bread and wine!" says that the inquirer may say, "I see something else, how is that you assert that I receive the body of Christ?" Ambrose then answers: "This is not what nature made, but what the blessing consecrated, and the power of blessing is greater than that of nature, because *by blessing nature itself is changed*" (*On the Mysteries* 8.48–49; my emphasis). Even more clearly in his *On the Christian Faith* he says, "by the mysterious efficacy of holy prayer [the elements] are transformed into the flesh and the blood" (4.10.125). As Barclay says the "idea of the conversion and transformation of the elements introduces a new epoch."[2] It should be stressed that we are not yet to the point of saying that doing the correct ritual will result in the transformation of the elements. It is clear that God or the Spirit in response to prayer causes the transformation.

It would not be long before some church fathers would try to answer the further question: how, more precisely, is this change brought about? Somewhere about A.D. 395, Gregory of Nyssa was to suggest that just as bread and wine, through the process of digestion became the actual body and blood of Jesus when the historical Jesus ate and drank them, so in the Eucharist the elements are immediately transformed by the action of the Logos (*Catechetical Oration* 37). This view was to triumph in the East, being affirmed by John of Damascus in 750 and many others thereafter.

This kind of "conversionist" explanation, however, did not satisfy some church fathers, particularly in the West. They continued to wonder, if a transformation had happened, how it still seemed, after the prayer, that these elements remained bread and wine. Augustine, followed by many thereafter, was to suggest that one should see the sacrament as having two natures just as Christ himself did. Augustine was to say that the sacrament of the Lord's Supper was "a visible sign of an invisible thing" (*De Cath. Rud.* 26.50). Ultimately this is where the still-current language about "an outward and visible sign of an inward and spiritual grace" comes from. Augustine is prepared to make a very clear-cut distinction. There is the *sacramentum*, which is the outward part, and there is the *res sacramenti* or the thing itself. Another way of putting this is to say there is a difference between the outward sacrament and its power.

Augustine is also the one who stresses that the sacrament is a Visible Word (see *Tract. In Joann.* 26.11–15 and 80.3). Augustine was to articulate clearly what previously may at best have only been implied by some church fathers—"It is not that which is seen that feeds, but that which is believed." "Believe and you have eaten" (*Sermon* 112.5; *Tract. In Joann.* 25.12). Without faith, one did not benefit from the sacrament. Augustine was also careful to distinguish between the physical and historical body of Jesus, which was not conveyed through the sacrament. It is rather the "essence" of his humanity, with the Spirit having quickened the sacramental elements, which one partakes of (*Tract. In Joann.* 17.5; 26.15). Notice as well Augustine is careful to say that even with the transformation of the elements, or perhaps one might say the activation of the invisible part of the sacrament, it was "a sacrament of commemoration of Christ's sacrifice" (*C. Faust.* 20.21), which only fully benefits those who believe.

The two major lines of the sacramental debate had been set up and would continue to be debated for centuries. In some ways the big debate took place in the ninth century between two monks with similar names—Radbertus and Ratramnus. What is so interesting about their debate is that they both claimed both Augustine and Ambrose for their cases. But as Ferguson says, "Radbertus used Ambrose to interpret Augustine, and Ratramnus used Augustine to interpret Ambrose on the Lord's Supper." Radbertus is important because in the middle of the ninth century he wrote what was the first full-length treatise on the Lord's Supper titled not accidentally *On the Body and Blood of the Lord*. He was not a Zwinglian before his time. He insisted that there was a real presence of the body and blood of Christ in the elements and that furthermore the body and blood in the Eucharist are identical with the body and blood of Jesus, the man who walked the earth and died on the cross.[3] Ratramnus, relying on the Augustinian distinction between the sacrament and the thing signified by the sacrament, stressed that one could not simply or fully identify the body of the historical Jesus with the mystical body of Christ in the sacrament. There is a resemblance between the two, but no identity statement can be made.

A real turning point came in the West, however, when a particular view was seen as heresy, the advocacy of which would have serious consequences. A teacher named Berengar of Tours, in about A.D. 1050, taught that there was no material change in the elements themselves but that inwardly to the mind they figured forth the body and blood of Christ, and after the consecration prayer the elements were or made available the spiritual body and blood of Christ on which the believer could feed. He also stressed that since the resurrection body of Christ was incorruptible and incapable of being broken into little pieces and chewed, it cannot be that body which is partaken of in the sacrament.

This sounded too much like no real change in the elements, and Pope Nicholas was not having it. Pressure was applied to Berengar, and he was forced to assent to the following statement from the Pope: "the bread and wine placed on the altar are after consecration not only a sacrament but also the true body and blood of our Lord Jesus Christ, and that these are sensibly handled and broken by the hands of the priests and crushed by the teeth of the faithful. Not only sacramentally but in reality." Berengar managed to raise the ire of yet another later pope, Pope Gregory the Seventh, and once more he was forced to assent that the elements underwent a substantial change, but now the statement read that the sacrament was transformed into "the real flesh of Christ which was born of the Virgin."[4]

Some will be surprised to learn that the term, and indeed the essential theology behind the term *transubstantiation* does not show up in the discussion before the twelfth century. Grounded in the Platonic distinction between universal ideas and their material copies called "accidents," the Schoolmen of this period made the distinction between the *substantia*, the invisible universal thing itself, and the *accidentia*, which are the sensible, tangible, visible properties that come into being when the universal takes on material form.

The idea of transubstantiation is that the *substantia* changed once consecrated, whereas the material *accidentia* remain the same. In A.D. 1215 the Fourth Lateran Council proclaimed, "His body and blood are really *contained* in the Sacrament of the altar under the species of bread and wine, the bread being transubstantiated into the body, and the wine into the blood, by the power of God." Aquinas (1225–1274) was to clarify some of the particulars of this position, which was to become the orthodox position of the Western church all the way up to the Reformation (and beyond). Aquinas stressed the real transformation of the *substantia*, while the accidents, which is to say the outward and material appearance of the sacrament, remained the same; otherwise, if the accidents themselves were changed, one would be actually eating and drinking human flesh and blood, and faith would be no longer a prerequisite to feeding on the Lord (*Summa Theol.* 3 Q. 65 Articles 2 and 4).

It was left to the Council of Trent to boldly claim what was absolutely untrue—"it has therefore *always* been held in the Church of God" that what Christ offered under the appearance of bread and wine was truly his body. In fact the matter had been under debate with varying views for centuries. But this same council was to introduce a further "official" development—namely the veneration of the elements themselves since they were believed to be the actual body and blood of Christ. The Council of Trent declaration *On the Worship and Veneration of the Holy Eucharist* was to claim, "And so no place is left for doubting that all Christ's faithful should in their veneration display towards this most Holy Sacrament the full worship of adoration which is due to the true God, in accordance with the custom *always received in the Catholic Church*" (my emphasis).[5]

We have come a very long way from that Passover meal in A.D. 30, and as one who believes that our doctrine should be grounded in the New Testament itself and its *clear* implications, this whole approach to the Lord's Supper is not merely a bridge too far—it is many bridges too far. It is in the first place the person of Christ, not his body parts, body and blood, that one worships if one is a Christian. More particularly, it is that union of the divine nature and human nature, making the risen Christ who he is, that we recognize. To worship even Christ's glorified human nature by itself, unless one wants to argue that it has been divinized (and so obliterate the two-natures theology of the earlier creeds) is completely inappropriate. God and God alone should be worshiped. The Bible is so very clear about this matter. Put another way, to worship Christ's glorified nature, his body for example, is to worship a thing—again, this is unfortunately idolatry or very nearly so.

Barclay, in a polemical passage, points out the things that followed from the doctrine insisted on at Trent:

> The priest simply by virtue of his ordination and apart altogether from his spiritual or moral quality was able to effect this change in the elements, which makes it a matter of magic rather than of religion. Into this there comes the conception of intention. That which was intended happens. Therefore, if the priest intended the sacrament for all, all receive it, irrespective of their faith or their life or spiritual condition. The grace of God operates mechanically in the sacrament for all who share in it. The idea that the elements change their substance and become the very substance of the body and blood of Christ makes the moment of consecration the most important moment in the whole sacramental service, and it begets an adoration and veneration of the elements themselves, which is not far short of idolatry. The very sacredness of the elements after this change make the taking of communion infrequent and did

much to bring about the withholding of the cup from the laity. This was the situation when the Reformation came to Europe.[6]

While this would not be a fair critique of a good deal of modern Catholic practice, it certainly is a fair critique of the Council of Trent and its pronouncements. The thing that remains amazing about that council is that various of its participants knew perfectly well that there had long been a variety of views on this contentious matter, and yet they presented their conclusions as if they went back to Jesus himself and were views the church had always held. This was frankly neither an honest nor a fair reading either of the New Testament or of earliest church history. But what would happen when Luther and his successors arose? To that we must now turn.

REHASHING THE MEAL—THE REFORMERS RETHINK

Sometimes the discussion of the Reformers begins and ends with Luther and Calvin, and perhaps Cranmer thereafter, but this is clearly a mistake. We must start before Luther and finish after the rise of the English Reformation to get the big picture. Already in 1379, John Wycliffe, rightly called the Morning Star of the Reformation, believing he was being true and faithful to what Augustine had suggested, rejected the doctrine of transubstantiation but not the idea of the spiritual presence of Christ, which can be perceived by faith alone. The bread and wine remained just bread and wine after consecration, and so he called them "sacramental signs." Wycliffe deemed it idolatry to identify the bread with the physical body of Christ.[7]

Though we are sometimes used to thinking that it was Luther who was the one who instituted the great reforms and was the seminal thinker, including on subjects like the Lord's Supper, it is clear enough that in fact Luther was heavily indebted to other reformers around him who also had problems with the doctrine of transubstantiation. Luther read with approval the works of Wessel Gansfort of the Netherlands and also Cornelius Hoen, a lawyer at the Hague. The former really is the font of the Protestant memorial view of the Lord's Supper, stressing that this was something we do in remembrance of Christ, and the latter, Hoen, stressed that John 6 and the words of institution no more were meant to be taken literally than when Jesus said he was the vine or the door. John 6 simply means that whoever believes in Christ partakes of the true bread who is Christ himself. Hoen says this was all spiritual language.

Martin Luther and Ulrich Zwingli were, of course, seminal figures in shaping the later Protestant views of the Lord's Supper. We need to bear in mind that they both were Catholic priests before they ever became Reformers, and this means that they had long celebrated the sacrifice of the Mass and had affirmed: (1) transubstantiation; (2) the distinction between substance and accidents; (3) the idea of the repetitive sacrifice of Christ upon the altar; (4) the real presence of Christ in the sacrament; and (5) the *ex opera operato* nature of the sacrament, namely that it happened automatically if the ritual was performed faithfully and correctly.

In 1520 Luther, in his seminal work *On the Babylonian Captivity of the Church* revealed that he had begun to change his mind on these things. In this work Luther claimed that for twelve hundred years the church had known nothing of the idea of transubstantiation, which in his usual subdued and subtle language Luther dubbed a monstrous idea in the form of a monstrous word (punning on the word monstrans/ monstrance referring to the altar vessel used to display the Eucharistic host). He attributed the idea to the pseudophilosophy of Aristotle's influence on the church in the previous three hundred years. He was likely mainly thinking of the influence on Aquinas, and it must be remembered that Luther had been an Augustinian monk. Luther discarded the notion of the sacrifice of the Mass, but he wanted to hold on to the real, even physical, presence of the Christ connected somehow with the sacrament. This led to the idea of consubstantiation, the presence of Christ somehow being attached to or under and with the sacramental elements. Luther clung then to a literal interpretation of "this is my body."

At the Colloquy of Marburg in 1529 it became apparent that Luther and Zwingli strongly disagreed on various aspects of the doctrine of the Lord's Supper. Interestingly, Zwingli made his arguments based on a close reading of the text of the Greek New Testament (remembering that Erasmus's Greek New Testament had appeared just a bit earlier in 1516), whilst Luther insisted they stick with the Latin or German. It looks like Zwingli had much the better of the argument, and unfortunately this event was to alienate the two Reformers thereafter, as they were both strong-willed men with tempers, and they argued vigorously and disagreed strongly on things like "the ubiquity of Christ's physical body" (a view that Luther held but Zwingli said was unbiblical).

Already by 1523 Zwingli had rejected the sacrifice of the Mass and had agreed with the statement "[t]hat Christ having sacrificed himself once, is in all eternity a true and sufficient sacrifice for the sins of all believers; therefore the mass is not a sacrifice but a thanksgiving memorial and an assurance of the forgiveness of sins."[8] By 1525 he was prepared to deny the real physical presence of Christ and speak of the spiritual presence of Christ with the Eucharist. He did not much like the word *sacramentum*, but it needs to be remembered that he did not see the Lord's Supper as a merely symbolic ceremony either. For those who received the elements in faith, there was the real spiritual presence of Christ, and Zwingli in addition was prepared to stress that there was communion not only with Christ, but that this ceremony involved fellowship within the community of faith. Marking this conceptual change, Zwingli got rid of the silver chalice, the monstrance, and instead went with wooden plates and wooden cups in an attempt to get back to a practice more like that of the New Testament times. The principle that Zwingli was to hold to, which became a watchword of the Anabaptist Reformers, was that everything must be tested by the Bible. This of course was to become the hallmark of the Protestant Reformation, and it was the engine driving the train of later thinking as well of Cranmer and Wesley about the sacraments. Perhaps what was most important that came out of the later Anabaptist discussion was that the Lord's Supper signified and celebrated the unique communion between the Lord and his people, and among believers as well. It did not just have a vertical dimension such that it was all about the individual believer's communion with the heavenly Christ.[9] We see here glimmerings of an approach that sounds far more like what Paul was talking about in 1 Corinthians 11 or Luke in Acts 2.

If we ask whether Thomas Cranmer or John Wesley really added much to these earlier Protestant discussions, if one allows that they both affirmed the spiritual presence of Christ with the Eucharist and were avid supporters of constant communion, not just sporadic taking of the Lord's Supper, because they saw it as a real means of grace, the answer is yes, at least in the case of Wesley. While early in his ministry in Georgia in the 1720s Wesley had upheld the principle of "fencing the Table of the Lord," the more mature Wesley's approach to the Lord's Supper involved the idea that while it was necessary to partake of the sacrament in a worthy manner, that nonetheless it could be a "converting" as well as a confirming or sanctifying sacrament since real grace was involved or conveyed spiritually. And so Wesley would allow anyone who was prepared to truly and earnestly repent of his or her sins to come and partake of the Lord's Supper "in both kinds." Wesley, then, took a broader view of the appropriate recipients of the Lord's Supper than many, as he saw it as a tool of evangelism, in essence. But Wesley also, being the high-church Anglican he was when it came to the sacraments, wanted the Lord's Supper to remain in the hands of the ordained clergy, hence the problems in America when there were so few ordained Methodists in the eighteenth and first half of the nineteenth centuries.

AND SO?

Much more could be said along these lines, but the important point is this: the Reformers realized that sacramental theology had strayed a very long way from the New Testament text and in various ways had betrayed its essence and character. It had abandoned the meal context, abandoned the *koinōnia* concept of "discerning that we are the body of Christ." It had turned the celebration of a miracle into something more like magic, and magic controlled by priests. There was of course to be a further and even more extreme reaction to Catholic and Orthodox theology in the form of low-church Protestant treatment of the Lord's Supper as entirely symbolic (and not symbols that participate in what they point to, but symbols that simply remind of something outside themselves), and even in some Quaker and other low-church circles there was the abandonment of the Lord's Supper almost altogether. Clearly enough, these extreme overreactions were equally violations of the spirit of a text like 1 Corinthians 11, in which Paul says that "whenever you come together," it should involve both a meal and the Lord's Meal as well.

In the next chapter we will see if we cannot craft both a theology and practice of the Lord's Supper that is faithful to the biblical witness without ignoring those traditions that properly amplify, explain, and carry forward the rather telegraphic and all-too-brief, relevant data in the New Testament itself. But it will be well to end this chapter with a reminder from Martin Marty: "The person who believes has what the words offer. Faith or belief is still another integral element in the Lord's Supper. The congregants are to cling to the words in faith and to receive the bread and wine in faith. This means they are to be serious people; God is making signs toward them. For them to fail to discern these signs and thus remain in unbelief is something for which they are held responsible."[10] Amen to that. Unbelief is unbelievable in a participant in the Lord's Supper.

Chapter 8

THE MYSTERY OF THE MEAL

What do we mean by the presence of Christ in this Supper? . . . Whoever studies this history of dispute over the sacrament or listens to present day theological debate might conclude that it is the number one issue. Why? Because it provides grist for intellectual debate and becomes a kind of test for people who like to sharpen their philosophical tools on things sacred. Being a historian of Christianity, I find it hard to look at the record without adding that if there is any feature of the Lord's Supper that brings out the meanest growls from partisan Christians, this is it. . . . The special problem with the presence of Christ in the Lord's Supper grows from the fact that the Scriptures are so nearly silent about it. This means that the Lord's Supper is used to fill in the blanks. Other teachings are like barnacles attached to it, and it gets connected to other doctrines.

—Martin Marty

We've all been there and done that. There are better and worse meals, memorable and eminently forgettable ones. But surely the Lord's Supper should be a memorable corporate act of the people of God. It should not be something done lightly or raced through quickly. Yet there have long been forces in Protestantism that have pushed many of us in that direction—toward really turning the Lord's Supper into fast food, the bread of haste indeed! Listen to the lament of Bishop Will Willimon:

> We got our recent custom of using individual glasses at Communion from Scotch [sic] Presybterians and others who, in order to recover the meal at the Lord's Supper, gave a communicant a glass of wine and a small bun, seated the congregations at tables, and had a meal which looked and tasted like a meal. The custom of using individual pressed white tasteless wafers is an extension of medieval preoccupations with the bread as a holy, untouched, spotless portion of Christ's body. Over the years both the glasses and the wafers got smaller until the church seemed to have a make-believe meal without food. . . .
>
> I finally said "enough is enough" a couple of years ago when I read of a man in the West, who, believing that the Lord's Supper is time consuming and cumbersome because of the individual cups involved, has begun marketing a product for those in a hurry. He produces airtight packets which contain a crackerlike pellet in one compartment and two grams of grape juice in another compartment—a disposable, self-contained, eat-on-the-run Lord's Supper—sort of "This is my body packaged for you." There you have it. The last hindrance to totally self-contained, self-centered religion is removed. . . . Now thanks to this unit packaging, we need never come into contact with or be touched by another human being again. Just when you thought modern life had depersonalized the gospel to the uttermost, we have another breakthrough—Communion without communion![1]

PICKING UP THE LEFTOVER FRAGMENTS

There is actually not that much debate about the Lord's Supper these days, even in very conservative circles. It is not one of the hot topics we find regular articles about in *Christianity Today* or *Interpretation* or *Christian Century*. In some ways, after one wades through the wreckage of centuries of hot dispute and then combs the field for useful fragments left over, one might expect that there's little of use for the twenty-first century church. Yet if we think this, we would be wrong, for postmoderns like mystery, and many are attracted to the church precisely because of its ritual, liturgy, and ceremony, especially if they are beautiful and move the emotions as well as appeal to the visual imagination. So perhaps we need to be like the disciples after the feeding of the five thousand and go back over the fields and pick up the leftover fragments. Who knows but that we may find many basketsful of serviceable food?

Let us start, then, with the primary part of the pasture we should be combing for nourishment—the Bible itself. It is hard to know how much of what we find, apart from the direct imperatives to "take and eat . . . and drink . . . and do this in remembrance . . ." are seen to be normative for the celebration of the Lord's Supper. It is one thing for a practice to have been normal in the first-century church, quite another for it to be normative today. And from a sociological point of view some of what was "normal" was a function of size more than commitment, and indeed of size more than culture.

There was a time when most Christians could cram themselves into a few homes and share everything in common. Those days are gone anywhere and everywhere except where the Christian population is very sparse or the situation is truly missional. One thing I have learned in my travels is that there are actually many places where it may appear there are no Christians, but in fact there are some, meeting clandestinely. A good example of this in the Middle East would be the "followers of Issah" in the Muslim world, found even in almost exclusively Muslim countries, with Issah being the Arabic name for Jesus. So, going forward in the twenty-first century we need to ask the right questions and be prepared to adopt and adapt practices to different cultural settings without losing the essence or core of the Lord's Supper. This is what the early church did when it adapted the

Passover meal, a Jewish meal, for the Greco-Roman setting of a *convivia* or *symposion*.

Should we recreate the Passover meal of the Last Supper? Actually there are some folks in conservative and particularly in messianic Jewish congregations doing this now. Yet it seems clear enough that the meal described as the Lord's Supper in 1 Corinthians is not merely a repetition of the Last Supper by any means, much less a mere repetition of the original Passover meal. In the Lord's Supper, for example, we do not have anyone playing the role of Judas at the meal, skulking out into the dark. The Lord's Supper is not a *reenactment* of the Last Supper in the same way that the Passover celebration is a bringing into the present of the Passover night in Egypt. There is not the same "we were there" element in the Lord's Supper celebration in the New Testament, so far as we can tell.

In fact, *the focus of the Lord's Supper is not on "the night when Jesus was betrayed"* but on the death of Jesus and its benefits. The liturgy begins by reminding the congregation of the night when Jesus was betrayed and what he said that night, but the actual focus is on the death of Christ on the cross and its benefits to believers. Having said this, it is well to caution that there is not a shred of evidence in the New Testament that the earliest celebration of the Lord's Supper was seen as a reenactment of the sacrifice on the cross any more than it was a reenactment of the Last Supper or the Passover. *Anamnesis*, remembering and cherishing and keeping in mind, not reenactment or re-presenting, is the character of this meal according to Paul. We share in this meal looking back and remembering Christ's once-for-all sacrifice and looking forward to his return. Christ's sacrifice is an unrepeatable, once-for-all event and neither should nor can be copied.

The focus of the original Lord's Supper *is not on the elements* in the present or the present in general, but on Christ and what he did and what he will do. It is Christ, not his parts, that we encounter at the Table, and partaking of the sacrament is a way of abiding in him as he abides in us. As Zwingli was to say, "this bread is my body" was not taken literally at the Last Supper or in the original Lord's Supper anymore than "I am the vine" was taken literally. This sort of language is typical ancient Jewish sapiential language where one thing is represented as another by means of analogy or a grand metaphor. The Lord's Supper is neither the Last Supper reenacted nor the Passover reenacted nor the messianic banquet yet to come, when we will sit down with Christ in the kingdom and many other strange and unexpected dinner guests. But it is well to recognize that there is a time limitation mentioned in the Lord's Supper. We only celebrate it "until he comes." It will be superceded by the messianic banquet one day.

Should we go back to having this meal in homes? Well, we could do this, but we would need to also then have worship in homes, and there is certainly nothing wrong with that. But the venue is not *mandated* in the New Testament, just the celebration.

Should we have the Lord's Supper in the context of a larger meal? Clearly this is how the earliest Christians did this, thus making it part of Christian hospitality in general. We have certainly lost a good deal of that welcoming feature of the meal. The Brethren do indeed celebrate the Lord's Supper in the context of the meal, but they do it in the fellowship hall, which means it tends to be separate from the main part of the worship. Perhaps the whole service could be held in the fellowship hall and the Lord's Supper be served in the context of a meal. This would take longer, but it would also add back the element of *koinōnia* and fellowship and sharing all things in common that originally characterized the meal.

It must be admitted that some of the modern adaptations of the Lord's Supper have in fact changed some important aspects of the original celebration and need to be changed back. There is absolutely no reason why real bread could not be used, and more importantly a whole loaf not yet broken, for the bread is in fact a double symbol, not only of Christ's own body, but of the church as the body of Christ—a united whole. This is surely what Paul has in mind in 1 Corinthians 10:17 when he says because we are one body we all partake of the one loaf. The meal is not meant just to unite us with Christ; it is also meant to unite us with one another, and this in part means that as we have been forgiven through Christ's death, we must also forgive one another. A story will illustrate my point.

At the end of the Civil War in Richmond, Virginia, on the Sunday after Appomattox and the surrender, a worship service was held in the historic Episcopal church there. It was an old church that had a balcony where the slaves of the owners had sat for many years, with their masters and their families sitting downstairs. The practice in this church had been to have two calls for the Lord's Supper, one first for the whites downstairs, and then one for the slaves upstairs. But on this given Sunday at the first call to communion an older black man, a former slave, began down the central aisle, right after the call. Naturally enough there was surprise and shock downstairs, but what was even more of a shock was when an elderly, white, bearded gentleman got up, hooked his arm in the arm of the former slave, and they went forward and took communion together. That man was Robert E. Lee. There was forgiveness and healing and reunion at the Table that day, and thereafter there was no more segregated communion. This is indeed one of the functions of communion—the receiving and sharing of forgiveness. Jesus sacrificed himself so that our sins might be forgiven and so that we might be forgiving as well.

Is the Lord's Supper a funerary or mere memorial meal, just remembering the past? Clearly enough, the early Christians did not see the meal in that sort of somber light. They did not celebrate the meal by having a picnic at a tomb. Rather it seems from 1 Corinthians 11 to have been a joyful and even raucous occasion, such that Paul had to warn against getting drunk or gluttony. The Lord's Supper was part of a feast, not a memorial fast. And here is where one of the real difficulties lies with modern practice of this sacrament.

By using tiny little wafers or miniscule morsels of hard cracker or bread already broken or baked in individual-sized portions, we totally lose two aspects of the symbolism—*we lose the sense that what we partake of and what we are is originally part of the "one loaf" we are now breaking and sharing with one another. We also lose the whole sense that it is food, and part of a meal.* God help us if we have any more guests who think we are serving snacks in the midst of a worship service! Anything that suggests "This is my snack given for you . . ." suggests something casual and trivial that makes a mockery of the sacrifice Christ made for us.

While the Lord's Meal should not be somber, it should be serious such that the elements themselves remind us that we are part of the body of Christ, and also that we are abiding in him and he in us. If we take a casual approach, we will not be encouraging our people to either "discern the body" and their part in it, or to partake in a worthy manner. I agree with John Westerhoff when he says "the Lord's Supper has a victorious redemptive focus more than a somber, funereal penitential one. The early Christians celebrated their sacred meal on Sunday—the Lord's Day, the day of victorious resurrection. Those who are gathered around the The Lord's Table might have been sinners, but they were *redeemed* sinners."[2]

If the Lord's Supper was not and is not merely symbolic in character, what is the spiritual transaction that happens at this meal? This of course is the age-old question we are still debating. On the one hand, Paul's solemn reminder in 1 Corinthians 11 that some have become sick and even died because of failure to "discern the body" makes clear this is a serious spiritual matter not to be taken lightly or blown off as a mere ritual or bunch of meaningless symbols. It is an occasion when one not only remembers that Jesus shared a meal with his disciples, but approaches this meal in a worthy manner, which I take to mean realizing that this is *our occasion to share a meal with Jesus.* He is the unseen host of this meal (and the elements should not be called the host!). He promised to be present wherever two or more are gathered.

In other words, I would suggest that we think back to the Emmaus Road story in Luke 24. Jesus became known to the two disciples in the breaking of the bread. It was the real risen Christ who was there with them in person. Indeed, he was the host of the meal. Listen to the story:

> As they sat down to eat, he took a small loaf of bread, asked God's blessing on it, broke it, then gave it to them. Suddenly their eyes

were opened and they recognized him. . . . They said to each other, 'Didn't our hearts feel strangely warm as he talked with us on the road and explained the Scriptures to us?' (30-32 NLT)

The Lord's Supper should be seen as a chance for a close encounter with Jesus, a chance for a moment of clarity and recognition in one's life that Christ comes to meet us, bless us, forgive us, over and over again, and that *we can and must actively participate in this joyful event.* It's not about magical rituals or medicinal elements; it's about the living presence of Christ, which can either be honored or dishonored by how we partake of the Meal. Yes, indeed a spiritual transaction happens at the meal, and it can be positive, and it can be negative. The real spiritual presence of Christ meets us at and in the Meal if we receive him by faith.

Is the Lord's Supper only for Christians? Whenever I ask this question I immediately remember the character of those that partook of the Last Supper with Jesus. They were certainly Jews, some better Jews than others, but Jesus shared this meal knowingly even with Judas. Or again consider the Emmaus Road encounter. Jesus shares this meal with those who had given up on his being the One to redeem Israel, who were leaving Jerusalem downcast and disappointed, and who were oblivious to the fact that it was Jesus who was speaking and sharing with them! There has to be a balance in the liturgy to help the congregation make a decision if they themselves are ready to partake of this Meal in a worthy manner (hence the "ye who do truly and earnestly repent" clause), while at the same time joyfully welcoming all who are willing and ready and able to do so.

The Lord's Supper is an active sacrament; it requires active participation of taking, eating, drinking. It is not for those who can't participate in it actively. They must be able to respond to the command to personally take it and eat it, and more importantly they must be able to discern both the body of believers around them and that this is a corporate, not an individual, act and to discern as well that they are meeting the unseen Host, Jesus himself, at the Table. In other words, a modicum of faith or receptivity is required to worthily participate in this Meal.

I have had church members who would not participate because they did not think they were worthy of doing so. I have had to remind them that it's not about *their* being worthy—Christ is the only worthy one; it's about them willingly participating in a way that honors Christ. That implies repentance of sins and a willingness to be forgiven and to forgive. But this reminder must be made to one and all. As N. Westerhoff says, "the Lord's Supper or Eucharist is primarily a corporate and communal act of worship. It is an occasion for community and communion rather than a time for a personal, private meeting with God. In that regard the Lord's Supper is a family meal."[3] This calls into question private communion, or a private taking of the Lord's Supper without the congregation—at a marriage ceremony for instance.

Some attention must be given to the differences between baptism and the Lord's Supper in this discussion. The prerequisites for the former are not the same as the prerequisites for the latter. Baptism is a passive sacrament, something done for the individual, and it is very much focused on the individual being baptized as he or she undergoes the initiation rite that symbolizes crossing the line into the new-covenant community. As a rite of passage, it is a once and once-only experience, which is why in Ephesians it can be said to be "one."[4]

The Lord's Supper, however, is different. It is a community ritual meant for the community to take together signifying their unity with Christ and with one another in and as the body of Christ. It is something one must be able to actively partake of, responding to the imperatives to take and eat and drink and "do this in remembrance," which requires conscious reflection. This means, I think, that while families should certainly bring their little children and infants to the Table, the appropriate thing to do is to bless them rather than serve them the elements until they can consciously respond to the imperatives freely and willingly on their own, with some beginnings of understanding of what they are doing. On the other hand, I quite agree with Wesley that we need to allow individuals themselves to be prompted by the Spirit and so allow them to do their own policing. The minister is not called upon to fence the table, but rather to call the family of faith to dinner. I also agree with Wesley that the Lord's Supper can become the occasion of conversion, and I don't say this because I think one automatically gets a dose of grace with the sacrament.

Are doses of grace conveyed through the partaking of the Lord's Supper? Had we asked Paul this question, I suspect he would have reminded us that: (1) God's grace is neither confined to nor contained within the material elements; (2) nothing is said in the New Testament about the elements being means of grace; but (3) God is gracious, and indeed Christ meets us when we commune with Him. In other words, without a theology of sacramental grace or grace conveyed through a sacrament, Paul would nonetheless not deny that a spiritual transaction can happen at the Table for those who commune in faith. It does not happen automatically or because the elements are somehow magically transformed into something more than bread or wine.

Should we use real bread and real wine, or are close substitutes adequate? My answer to this is that it would be better if we used the same elements as were used originally. This at least provides some continuity with New Testament practice. A real loaf of fresh bread (whether leavened or unleavened does not much matter) and preferably real wine (there is nonalcohol communion wine for those denominations whose members are teetotalers, a wine that is more than grape juice and less than Gallo). It has sometimes been joked about my denomination (Methodist) that Jesus turned the water into wine at Cana, and we have been busily reversing the process ever since. It is right to note that were the wine not alcoholic at the Christian meal, Paul's warnings against drunkenness at the meal in 1 Corinthians 11 would have been pointless indeed. It is also right to note that at the normal meal and symposium in the Greco-Roman world they did in fact water down the wine, though the reason for doing so was so they could drink more! I honor those traditions that know very well the dangers of alcoholism rampant in our culture and do not want to cause their weaker brothers and sisters to stumble at the Lord's own Table. For them, partaking of the Lord's Supper with alcoholic wine could indeed be partaking in an unworthy manner that does them harm. If the celebration at the Lord's Supper is meant to be for the corporate body of Christ, that should include even those who have no tolerance for alcohol.

Bread and wine were the ordinary staples of everyday life in Jesus' and Paul's world. When we partake of the Lord's Supper, we are reminding ourselves of the Lord's Prayer, "give us this day our daily bread." We are reminding ourselves that all good gifts come from God. "Christianity is a 'materialistic' faith. The ordinary, familiar, basic stuff of everyday life—bread and wine—opens up new levels of communion with the Divine in our midst. All of our senses are engaged in this multi-media, sensuous, multi-facteted experience of the divine-human encounter."[5] At the Lord's Table we are bidden, "taste and see that the Lord is good," not "taste and see the elements which have become the Lord are good" (sadly, sometimes they are more like cardboard even when partaken of by faith).

Does the time of day or the time in the service make a difference in regard to when we commune? In the first place, it is true to say that Paul expects that whenever the whole body comes together, there should be a Lord's Supper as part of the act of worship. This is reasonably clear from 1 Corinthians 11. That was Paul's normal expectation though he falls short of making it normative. In my view it would be better if we did indeed celebrate the Lord's Table whenever we all gather together. Of course the early Christians basically met in homes and at night, and that too, while normal, was not made normative. I must say though that there is something special about a Vespers communion service, or a candlelight communion service. For one thing, it's closer to dinner time! And the Lord's Supper was not meant to be "the Lord's light breakfast." It would indeed be better if it were held in the evening and was indeed a part of a regular meal. Then it would do a better job of reminding us we are the Lord's family and we share in a family meal together.

When I was growing up, we used to go to church on Wednesday night for what were called "wonderful Wednesdays." We would share a meal, often share communion, there would be singing of hymns (I don't remember an offering however), and there would be an after-dinner speaker, usually a minister. After that we would go to various programs or meetings for an hour or so. It was a grand time. The initial event transpired in the fellowship hall. Worship and fellowship happened together. I look back on that and think this was as close as we ever got to worshiping like the early Christians, and how good it was indeed. We need to find a time and a way, an evening time and a way, perhaps, to manage to do this again.

Who should serve the Lord's Supper? Well in the early church, considering Acts 2 and 1 Corinthians 11, the host of the home presumably was the host of the meal, and as I have said, really, the Lord is the host at his own Table, not any of us. We are all just participants, we are all celebrants. I don't think there is any biblical warrant for the serving of the Lord's Supper to be confined to ministers, but I do think that anyone who undertakes such a sacred task should be trained to do it in a respectful manner.

Let me sum up. There are better and worse ways to share in the Lord's Supper. It is not itself a sacrifice or a Mass, it does not require priests; it is not a repetition of the Last Supper, or Passover, or of repeatable Old Testament sacrifices, or a reenactment of Jesus' death on the cross. As we pointed out earlier, in the Old Testament sacrifices the people themselves brought the sacrifice to the altar, not the priests. In other words, even on an Old Testament model, the action was not reserved to clerics. Practices that suggest something automatically or magically happens to the elements due to the ritual or due to a prayer probably have no basis in the New Testament. There is nothing in the gospels or the rest of the New Testament to suggest that when Jesus prayed, this act consecrated the elements of the meal. He was simply giving thanks to God who brings forth bread from the earth, as was the traditional Jewish thing to do. Therefore, all this heat and debate about what happens at the prayer of consecration is probably much ado about not very much. Prayer in the Lord's Supper consecrates us and prepares all of us to partake of the meal in a worthy manner, as we bow before the giver of all good gifts. "We do not presume to come to this thy table . . ." is a good prayer to pray on the way to the Table as it prepares us. The Lord and his body needs no preparation. He is ready and waiting at the Table.

All other things being equal, we should share in this family meal as often as we can, binding ourselves together and to our Lord. Our world, and indeed the church, is so fragmented that we need every possible means of overcoming our disunity and dysfunctionality, and the Lord's Supper regularly shared is one such means.

There is of course a danger in making too little or too much of the Lord's Meal. To judge from 1 Corinthians 11–14, the Lord's Supper took up less time than the worship acts that followed it as mentioned in 1 Corinthians 14. It was not the centerpiece of worship, but it also was not an afterthought, as sometimes becomes the case when we simply have "closing" communion, or even communion after the service in a nearby chapel. The latter ceases to be an act of corporate or whole-body worship. And a closing communion hastily run through does no honor or service to the worship service. The dramatic reading out of Paul's letters seems to have been a major and regular part of worship then—call it a sermon. This would certainly have taken much longer than the Lord's Supper ceremony in the midst of the meal. But again the New Testament does not tell us anywhere how long to linger on each of these aspects of worship. What we must do is do them well, and often. And there is no better day to gather at the risen Lord's Table than on his day, the day of resurrection, the Lord's Day.

I must share two more stories with you as we draw to a close. I have a dear friend in Turkey who is my tour guide. Her name is Meltem, which means "breeze." She came with me and my group to Israel for the first time in the summer of 2006 and was very excited. Near the end of our time in Jerusalem, we went to the Garden Tomb to take communion. Mel had already asked me if a Muslim who loves Jesus could be baptized in the Jordan, and I quite naturally said yes. On this communion Sunday, as all my tour group was coming forward to commune, I could see her hanging back with tears in her eyes. She knew what was happening, and she longed to be part of the body, part of the Supper on that day, so I motioned for her to come forward and share in communion with us all. We indeed as a whole group on that Sunday were all one, as he is One. It was a day I will never forget. Special things happen at the Lord's Table, people even coming to Christ for the first time.

It was the end of another tour several years prior, and we were finishing on a Sunday in Rome in the catacombs. It was a hot early evening in August, but we were descending about 150 feet down into the cool earth of the catacombs. Our guide, Georgio, by his own admission a lapsed Catholic, was with us. The barrel-vaulted ceiling in this catacomb resounded with our singing of "Let us Break Bread Together," and as the ceremony transpired, I could see Georgio weeping, weeping over his sins and spiritual estrangement from Christ. Of course I welcomed him to the table. It was an awesome thing to stand in a room where Christian martyrs had once been laid to rest and to stare at the now empty niches and to sing "For all the Saints who from their labors rest / Who thee by faith before the world confessed / Thy name O Jesus, be forever blessed. . . . Alleluia."

That day a prodigal came at least part of the way home, and we all felt we were communing not merely with those physically present but with the whole company of heaven. As the Shakers suggest, when we invite people to the Lord's Table we should say, "We make ye kindly welcome. . . ." The Lord's Supper is all about Christian hospitality, in part because the church itself is the Lord's hospital, the place where we come to be cured of our sin sickness.

The Lord's Supper was originally used as a destratifying tool by Paul. He wanted less hierarchy and pecking order, and more equality amongst the participants. One wonders indeed how happy he would be that in so many Christian contexts today the meal is controlled by clerics who not only control and perform the ritual, but usually serve themselves first and others later, ignoring the complaint of Paul about the well-to-do and the poor in Corinth! Protestants like to say we all stand on level ground at the cross, for we are all equal at the foot of the cross. I would add we are all supposed to be equal when we kneel or sit at the Lord's Table as well. The leveling effect of the Meal needs to come more into play in some quarters these days.

So too does its declaratory nature. By this I mean that the Meal is one way we proclaim Christ's death until he comes. The regular sharing of this meal should provide ample opportunities for reflection and preaching on the dead-but-risen Christ. The Word made Visible should be coupled with the Word made audible. There is too little good teaching these days on the atoning sacrifice of Christ, once for all time and all persons. A renewal of good sacramental practice should be accompanied by a renewal of good preaching on the substance and focal subject of the Lord's Supper—the Lord himself and his salvific work.

Someday, when we all sit down at the messianic banquet, we will know as we are known. We will know whether we have served at the Lord's Table well or poorly, whether we have welcomed the right participants or not, viewed the elements right or not, done it often enough or not, remembered the right things or not, partaken in a worthy manner or not, properly honored Christ's death until he comes or not. It was John Calvin who rightly said about the Lord's presence in or with the Eucharist: "I would rather experience it than understand it."[6] It was Charles Wesley who sang:

> Who shall say how bread and wine
> God into man conveys?
> How the bread his flesh imparts,
> How the wine transmits his blood,
> Fills his faithful people's hearts,
> With all the life of God?
> Sure and real is the grace,
> The manner be unknown;
> Only meet us in thy ways,
> And perfect us in one.

Let us taste the heavenly powers Lord,
We ask for nothing more.
Thine to bless, 'tis ours,
To wonder and adore.[7]

Someday the currently invisible Host will show up, and we will see him face to face. It is a consummation devoutly to be wished. In the meantime, we must learn to be better dinner guests, waiting on one another, communing together with one eye on heaven and one on each other. We need to relearn how to make a meal of it rather than a mess of it, as we so often do. The Lord's Supper is all about love, Christ's great love for us, which is why it was originally part of a meal called an *agapē*. It was once said "I asked Jesus how much he loved me, and he stretched out his arms wide and died."[8] I would say we need to stretch out our arms wide and welcome the congregation all to the Table. I leave you with one of my poems I wrote for the Lenten season long ago:

RSVP

To move from fast to feast,
From ashes to riding an ass,
From wilderness wandering
God's willingness wondering
To follow the way of the cross
To find what was utterly lost—
   All this was Lent to us.

The cup not passed over
By our Passover
The vinegar he willingly drank—
But through gift divine
New covenant wine

Came forth from his side as he sank—
    All this was given to us.

Through breaking of bread
They knew their head
The joy of new life begun
From out of the depths,
From out of his death
His people one loaf had become—
    All this was food for us.

Lent leads to Easter
The faster turns feaster
A foretaste for those in the dust
A bread with new leaven
The manna from heaven—
    All this has risen for us.

God's ways are not our ways,
Our eyes cannot see
The logic of love,
Nailed to a tree.
Come now to the dinner
Come saint and come sinner—
    The meal is now served to us.

—Lent 1982

NOTES

Chapter 1

1   B. Childs, *The Book of Exodus: A Critical Theological Commentary* (Philadelphia: Westminster, 1974), 207.

2   See Joachim Jeremias, *The Eucharistic Words of Jesus* (London: SCM Press, 1966).

3   One wonders if there were early slogans like "Nisan saves."

4   On which see volume 1 in this brief trilogy—*Troubled Waters.*

5   Some of this material appears in another form in my article "Making a Meal of It: The Lord's Supper in its First-Century Social Setting," in *The Lord's Supper: Believers' Church Perspectives*, ed. Dale. R. Stoffer (Scottsdale Pa.: Herald Press, 1997), 81–113, and 304–11 for the notes. See Jerome Neyrey, "Ceremonies in Luke-Acts: The Case of Meals and Table Fellowship," in *The Social World of Luke-Acts*, ed. Jerome Neyrey (Peabody, Mass.: Hendrickson, 1991), 361–87.

6   Mary Douglas, "Deciphering a Meal," in *Implicit Meanings: Essays in Anthropology* (London: Routledge, 1975), 249–75, here 249.

7   I am of course alluding to the famous conference at Worms (pronounced Vorms, like forms), which helped further spur the Lutheran Reformation and Luther's own reflections on the Lord's Supper. The exact content of what Luther said at that meeting is debated, especially in regard to his supposed, most-famous remark—"Here I stand, I can do no other." See Roland H. Bainton's famous life of Luther, *Here I Stand: A Life of Martin Luther* (Nashville: Abingdon), 1990.

Chapter 2

Epigraph. Christine Pohl, *Making Room: Recovering Hospitality as a Christian Tradition* (Grand Rapids: Eerdmans, 1999), 17.

1   Jeremias, 27.

2   Philip R. Davies, George J. Brooke, and Phillip R. Callaway, *The Complete World of the Dead Sea Scrolls* (London: Thames & Hudson, 2002), 202.

3   Maurice Casey, *Aramaic Sources of Mark's Gospel* (Cambridge: Cambridge University Press, 1999), 219–52.

4   On all of this compare Ben Witherington III, *The Gospel of Mark: A Social-Rhetorical Commentary* (Grand Rapids: Eerdmans, 2001).

5   Jeremias, 204.

6   Jeremias, 220, and 220 on the translation.

7   Jeremias, 224.

8   See Ben Witherington III, *The Acts of the Apostles* (Grand Rapids: Eerdmans, 1998), 157–59.

9   See Brian Capper, "The Palestinian Cultural Context of Earliest Christian Community of Goods," in *The Book of Acts in its Palestinian Setting* (Grand Rapids: Eerdmans, 1995), ed. R. J. Bauckham (vol. 4 of *The Book of Acts in Its First-Century Setting*), 323–56.

10   Capper, 325 nn. 3 and 5.

11   Capper, 343.

12   See the discussion in Witherington, *Acts of the Apostles*, 159–61.

Chapter 3

Epigraph. Ramsay MacMullen, *Roman Social Relations 50 B.C. to A.D. 284* (New Haven: Yale University Press, 1974), 76.

1 See the volume *Dining in a Classical Context* (Ann Arbor: University of Michigan Press, 1991), ed. W. J. Slater, particularly the article by Walter Burkett, "Oriental Symposia: Contrasts and Parallels," 7–24, esp. 18.

2 Kathleen E. Corley, "Were the Women around Jesus Really Prostitutes? Women in the Context of Greco-Roman Meals," *SBL 1989 Seminar Papers*, ed. David J. Lull (Atlanta: Scholars Press, 1989), 487–521, here 513.

3 See the extended discussion in Ben Witherington III, *Conflict and Community in Corinth: A Socio-Rhetorical Commentary on 1 and 2 Corinthians* (Grand Rapids: Eerdmans, 1994). 221–32.

4 Ramsay MacMullen, *Paganism in the Roman Empire* (New Haven: Yale University Press, 1981), 40.

5 See my discussion in "Not So Idle Thoughts about *Eidolothuton*," *TynBul* 44.2 (1993): 237–54.

6 "Not So Idle," 237–54.

7 See J. Y. Campbell, "*Koinōnia* and its Cognates in the New Testament," *JBL* 51 (1932): 352–80, here 375–77.

8 G. D. Fee, *The First Epistle to the Corinthians* (Grand Rapids: Eerdmans, 1987), 469–70.

9 E. A. Judge, "The Social Identity of the First Christians," *JRH* 11 (1980): 201–17.

10 Stephen C. Barton, "Paul's Sense of Place: An Anthropological Approach to Community Formation in Corinth," *NTS* 32 (1986): 225–46.

11 MacMullen, *Roman Social Relations*, 73.

12 D. E. Smith, "Meals and Morality in Paul and His World," in *SBL 1981 Seminar Papers* (Scholars Press, 1981), 319–39, here 323.

13 Smith, 323.

14   Smith, 323.

15   Wayne A. Meeks, *The First Urban Christians: The Social World of the Apostle Paul* (New Haven: Yale University Press, 1983), 78–79.

16   Meeks, 78–79.

17   See pp. 121–25 below.

Chapter 4

1   For a more detailed treatment of this material see Ben Witherington III, *John's Wisdom: A Commentary on the Fourth Gospel* (Louisville, Ky.: Westminster John Knox, 1995).

2   Fred Craddock, *John* (Atlanta: John Knox, 1980), 100.

3   See Ramsay MacMullen, *Enemies of the Roman Order: Treason, Unrest, and Alienation in the Empire* (Cambridge: Harvard University Press, 1966), 59.

4   See now Ben Witherington III, *Letters and Homilies for Hellenized Christians*, vol. 2 (Downers Grove: InterVarsity, 2006) on the Johannine literature and its audience.

5   M. Oberweis, "Das Papias-Zeugnis vom Tode des Johannes Zebedai," *NovT* 38 (1996), 277–95.

6   See Richard Bauckham, *Jesus and the Eyewitnesses: The Gospels as Eyewitness Testimony* (Grand Rapids: Eerdmans, 2006).

7   Andrew Lincoln, *The Gospel According to Saint John* (Peabody, Mass.: Hendrickson, 2005), 22.

8   See Witherington, *John's Wisdom*.

9   If one makes this sharp a distinction and so sees the two separate stories stitched together at 13:18 by the saying of Jesus, then this would mean that the Beloved Disciple was in fact present at the Last Supper since he is said in 13:23 to be present at that meal as well.

10   D. A. Carson, *The Gospel According to John* (Grand Rapids: Eerdmans, 1991), 462–63.

11   Unless of course one sees the literal foot as a symbol of the figurative third foot, for in early Judaism the term foot was used to refer to the male genitals.

12   One may rightly wonder if there is a connection with the Lazarus who ends up in the bosom of Abraham in the parable in Luke 16:19-31.

Chapter 5

1   See William Brosend, *James and Jude* (Cambridge: Cambridge University Press, 2005), 178.

2   See *The Works of the Emperor Julian*, (Cambridge: Harvard University Press, 2005), LCL 3, 67–71. See the discussion in Pohl, 43–44.

3   See Ben Witherington III, *Letters and Homilies for Jewish Christians* (Downers Grove: InterVarsity, 2007), ad loc.

4   See I. H. Marshall, *Last Supper and Lord's Supper* (Grand Rapids: Eerdmans, 1980), 139–40.

5   Of the two long titles the former one is more likely to be original, especially since the Didache seems to be a Jewish Christian document, and the Twelve so far as we can tell did not as a group address Gentiles.

6   See the discussion of Bart Ehrman in *The Apostolic Fathers*, vol. 1 (Cambridge: Harvard University Press, 2003), 411–12. The reference to hills would seem to make Egypt a less likely choice for locale, though it has been suggested.

7   On which, see the first volume in this series—Ben Witherington III, *Troubled Waters: Rethinking the Theology of Baptism* (Waco: Baylor University Press, 2007), 88.

Chapter 6

Epigraph. William Barclay, *The Lord's Supper* (London: SCM Press, 1967), 56.

1   Barclay, 57.

2   Everett Ferguson, "The Lord's Supper: The Early Church through the Medieval Period," in *The Lord's Supper: Believers'*

Church Perspectives, ed. Dale. R. Stoffer (Scottsdale Pa.: Herald Press, 1997), 21–45, here 23.

3 See Ferguson's cautionary remarks, 24.

4 Ferguson, 25.

5 The comment on prophesy appears to be a later editorial comment inserted into the text.

Chapter 7

Epigraph. Pohl, 42–43.

1 Meeks, 159–60.

2 Barclay, 67.

3 Ferguson, 33.

4 This is all cited in Barclay, 70–71.

5 See Barclay, 73.

6 Barclay, 73–74.

7 See William R. Estep Jr., "Contrasting Views of the Lord's Supper in the Reformation of the Sixteenth Century," in *The Lord's Supper: Believers' Church Perspectives*, ed. Dale. R. Stoffer (Scottsdale Pa.: Herald Press, 1997), 46–62, here 48.

8 Estep, 54.

9 Estep, 61–62.

10 Martin Marty, *The Lord's Supper* (Minneapolis: Augsburg Fortress, 1997), 37.

Chapter 8

Epigraph. Marty, 72–73.

1 William Willimon, *Sunday Dinner: The Lord's Supper and the Christian Life* (Nashville: Upper Room, 1981), 103–4.

2 John Westerhoff, introduction to *Sunday Dinner*, by Willimon, 114.

3   Westerhoff, in Willimon, 113.
4   See Witherington, *Troubled Waters*.
5   Westerhoff, in Willimon, 113–14.
6   See Willimon, 29.
7   See the discussion in Willimon, 30.
8   Willimon, 89.

SCRIPTURE INDEX

EXTRA-BIBLICAL CHRISTIAN

GENERAL INDEX